D0726901

T.
ILLUSTRATED
BOOK OF
FILM LISTS

REES AND LAZELL

With an introduction by

Joel W Finler

Virgin Books

First published in Great Britain in 1982 by
Virgin Books Ltd, 61-63 Portobello Road,
London W11 3DD.

ISBN 0 907080 43 X

Printed and bound in Great Britain by
Richard Clay (The Chaucer Press) Ltd,
Suffolk.

Production services by Book Production
Consultants, Cambridge.

Designed by Ray Hyden.

Typeset by Laura Beck and Lynne Shippam
at Portobello Typesetting.

CONTENTS

THE COMPILERS

Barry Lazell and **Dafydd Rees** are the directors of the Media Research and Information Bureau (MRIB), a company which provides a variety of research and creative services to the publishing, music, broadcasting and other media industries. Their 'Rock Records: A Book of Lists' (companion to the present volume) and 'Chartfile 1982' (compiled with Alan Jones) have already been published by Virgin Books, and several other titles have been completed or are in preparation.

MRIB's work can also be found regularly in such journals as Sounds, Popular Video, Record Business, Music and Video Week, Record Mirror, Flexipop, What Video, and Noise. The origination and co-ordination of the HMV Shop Marathon Music Quiz, first broadcast by Radio 1 at Easter 1982, was also provided by MRIB.

The Lazell/Rees partnership was formed when both were founder members of the Record Business Research Department. Dafydd, resident in London, now directs operations from the company's Duke Street offices; Barry divides his time between his desk in the West End and his typewriter in mid-Essex.

WITH THANKS

The information contained in the lists in this book has inevitably come from a wide variety of sources. The compilers must first acknowledge several standard works of reference on the cinema, to which extensive reference has been made for basic facts — and which often provided points of inspiration for off-beat lists which might have surprised the original writers! Our thanks, then, to the work of Leslie Halliwell (author of 'Film Guide', 'Filmgoer's Companion' and 'Filmgoer's Book of Quotes'), Ephraim Katz (author of the 'Film Encyclopaedia'), and all the other authors whose reference books passed across our desks.

Many of the charts, figures and tables concerning box office stars and money-making films are adaptations of facts and figures to be found in journals serving the film industry. Particular acknowledgement must go here to Quigley Publications for the star ratings, and to 'Variety' for the financial information.

Several individuals must be noted, particularly Joel Finler, who lent not only his help, advice and encyclopaedic knowledge of the movies, but whose resources are almost entirely responsible for the pictorial content of the book. MRIB's own Luke Crampton lent much elbow grease and telephone time, Virgin's Robert Devereux directed the whole operation with De Mille-like zeal (and occasional brimstone), and the book's designers have done their customary eye-opening job with the material we brought to them.

Organisations without whose co-operation this book could not have existed include BAFTA, the British Film Institute, the Academy of Motion Picture Arts and Sciences and, above all, the film companies whose stills provide the bulk of the illustrations: 20th Century Fox, Columbia Pictures, EMI Films, Lucasfilm, Metro-Goldwyn-Mayer, Paramount Pictures, J Arthur Rank Productions, United Artists, Universal Pictures, Walt Disney Productions, and Warner Brothers. We particularly appreciated the helpful co-operation of the London Press Office of Walt Disney Productions. Most of the portrait and behind-the-camera shots used in the book are from the collection of Joel Finler.

Every attempt has been made to contact holders of copyright material reproduced in this book, and any infringement of copyright is accidental. In the case of any question arising out of the use of copyright material, the author will be pleased to make the necessary corrections in any further editions of the book.

Barry Lazell and Dafydd Rees

PREFACE

The world of the movies, by virtue of its glamour, its mystique, its associations with big money, fantasy and wish-fulfilment, has been a subject of constant fascination to those of us on the outside ever since it sprang up as an entertainment medium at the beginning of the Century. Through the decades when the silver screen was the pre-eminent form of popular entertainment, and 'going to the pictures' probably the major social activity, the people who created the movies — and particularly those who starred in them — became the folk heroes of the age. They were followed and adored through every move they made, either on or off screen, in what was most certainly the first demonstration of the now-familiar phenomenon of fan worship.

Likewise, through those same years, the films in which those adored stars featured became the surrogate mass-appeal literature of an era brought low successively by depression and war. The movies were the great means of escapism; small wonder that their appeal took on a fascination which has never entirely waned.

Even today, when cinema has been eclipsed as a mass medium by television and other forms of domestic entertainment, the movies can still pull off their wondrous tricks, inaugurating fads, fashions and whole new cultural spin-offs with as much ease as their flickering black-and-white forebears. If this seems doubtful, just look at the impact which 'Star Wars' has made upon our popular culture in every area from film technology to children's toys, and think again.

This book does not pretend to be a history of the cinema, a study of the objectives of film or the intentions of their makers. It does not set out to study the movies in a critical sense; we may make critical judgements here and there, but these should be taken within the context of our explanatory annotations, and certainly not as points for learned discussion.

What we have attempted to do is to draw out the areas of fascination in the cinema — the award winners, the financial successes, the biggest stars, the interesting directors, and above all the areas of sheer trivia which — as in all areas of entertainment — people love to see categorised, and not so much dissected as assembled for the fan's-eye view. Hence there are lists here for all tastes: the historical, the humorous, the revealing and the purely entertaining. We hope we have presented you with a volume you can pick up and put down, skim through or read cover to cover, hopefully finding something new to catch your interest at every turn.

BARRY and DAFYDD, MRIB

INTRODUCTION

It is appropriate that a book of movie lists should start with the Oscar winners. As the longest established and best known of film awards — with an unbroken run stretching from the late silent era up to the present day — the Oscars reflect the changes that have taken place in the cinema over a period of more than half a century. And they provide a useful basis for comparison with the other lists and information in the pages which follow.

Not surprisingly, a large number of the top Oscar winners have rated highly at the box office ranging from 'Broadway Melody' to 'Ben Hur' and from 'Gone With the Wind' to 'The Godfather' and 'Rocky' during the 1970s. Universal's 'The Sting' in 1973 was the studio's first Best Oscar winner for 43 years and its biggest money-maker ever until the arrival of 'Jaws' two years later.

Boasting of "more stars than there are in heaven", MGM dominated the acting awards during the early sound era and on through the 1930s. The rapid growth of Columbia and United Artists to major status for the first time during the 1950s is clearly reflected in their Oscar successes with such pictures as 'On the Waterfront', 'Marty', 'Around the World in 80 Days' and 'The Bridge on the River Kwai', and the companies were becoming more international at the same time.

The introduction of the British Film Academy awards from 1946 drew attention to the quality of the post-war British cinema and some of the best pictures coming from the Continent like 'Bicycle Thieves' and 'Jeux Interdits'. And the acting awards gave recognition to many of the top British actors like Peter Finch, Trevor Howard, Peter Sellers and Ralph Richardson who were not even nominated for an Oscar during the 1960s.

A few surprises can be found in the book, like 'The Third Man', 'Help!' and 'Monty Python's Life of Brian' among the top money-making films in Britain, although this list has been dominated by the James Bond cycle during recent years.

Kenneth Anger in his book *Hollywood Babylon* accuses Quigley (of the Motion Picture Herald and Almanac) of fabricating a "bogus blacklist" of stars who were box office Poison. But the listings of Top Box Office Stars appear to be a fair indication of the drawing power of such stars as Shirley Temple at Fox during the 1930s or Bing Crosby at Paramount in the 1940s as well as John Wayne slightly later and Clint Eastwood during more recent years. However, they do not indicate the extraordinary achievement of someone like Mae West who singlehandedly, as scriptwriter and star, saved Paramount from bankruptcy in 1933 with smash hits for her first two starring films.

In recent years the top hits like 'Star Wars' and 'Close Encounters' have not been Oscar winners, although they have been honoured by the Academy for their remarkable cinematography, special effects and technical expertise. Since film making is a collaborative art, one of the important functions performed by the Oscar and Bafta awards is to recognise such achievements, too. Perhaps one needs a second volume to include lists of the outstanding writers, cameramen, art directors and others — those relatively unknown men and women who have played such an important role in the story of the cinema from its inception up to the present day.

JOEL W FINLER

THE ACADEMY AWARD WINNERS

In 1927, after several incidents had seriously tainted Hollywood's reputation, the film industry founded the Academy Of Motion Pictures Arts And Sciences. Its purpose was to raise the cultural, educational and scientific standards of film. The Academy had 36 original members, with Douglas Fairbanks Sr. as its first president. In order to further increase its new-found credibility, it also announced the introduction of its annual achievement awards. These were first presented on May 16th 1929 in a ceremony at the Hollywood Roosevelt Hotel, before 250 people. The achievements honoured covered the period from August 1927 to July 1928. Subsequent ceremonies have been held annually each April since then, honouring cinematic achievements of the past year.

The origin of the word 'Oscar' still remains in doubt. Until 1931 it was known simply as 'The Statuette', and how the new name came about depends upon which story you believe. Hollywood columnist Sidney Skolsky says he made it up because he simply got tired of referring to The Statuette. The story attributed to Bette Davis is that she named it after her first husband, Harmon Oscar Nelson Jr. Perhaps the most likely explanation, however, is that of the Academy Librarian, Margaret Herrick, who had remarked of the statuette that "He looks like my Uncle Oscar." The figure, standing 13½ inches high and made of gold-plated bronze, is of a man with a sword standing on a reel of film. MGM art director Cedric Gibbons designed the original, and sculptor George Stanley was paid five thousand dollars to cast the first figure, which was of gold-plated Brittania metal.

Marlon Brando

ACADEMY AWARD WINNERS

Best Picture

(Listings show film title, director (bracketed) and main stars)

1927/8 **WINGS** *(William Wellman)*
CHARLES ROGERS, CLARA BOW, RICHARD ARLEN
A silent about the pioneer fliers of the 1st World War, which also gained an award for Roy Pomeroy's 'Engineering Effects'.

1928/9 **THE BROADWAY MELODY** *(Harry Beaumont)*
ANITA PAGE, BESSIE LOVE
One of the original sound musicals, originator of a staple genre of the 30s and 40s.

1929/30 **ALL QUIET ON THE WESTERN FRONT** *(Lewis Milestone)*
LEW AYRES, LOUIS WOLHEIM, SLIM SUMMERVILLE
The classic World War 1 drama adapted from Erich Maria Remarque's novel of the same title.

1930/1 **CIMARRON** *(Wesley Ruggles)*
RICHARD DIX, IRENE DUNNE
Western about the opening of the Cimarron Strip, from a novel by Edna Ferber.

1931/2 **GRAND HOTEL** *(Edmund Goulding)*
GRETA GARBO, JOAN CRAWFORD, LIONEL BARRYMORE, JOHN BARRYMORE
The first multi-starred Oscar winner, adapted from Vicki Baum's novel of the same title.

1932/3 **CAVALCADE** *(Frank Lloyd)*
CLIVE BROOK, DIANA WYNYARD
A Noel Coward spectacular which also won Oscars for director Lloyd and its art director William Darling.

1934 **IT HAPPENED ONE NIGHT** *(Frank Capra)*
CLARK GABLE, CLAUDETTE COLBERT
A romantic comedy which also won Oscars for its director *and* both the male and female co-stars.

1935 **MUTINY ON THE BOUNTY** *(Frank Lloyd)*
CLARK GABLE, CHARLES LAUGHTON
The famous true story of an 18th Century Naval incident, with Laughton in one of his most celebrated roles as Captain Bligh.

1936 **THE GREAT ZIEGFELD** *(Robert Z. Leonard)*
WILLIAM POWELL, LUISE RAINER
A mammoth three-hour spectacular musical biography of the Broadway showman. Seymour Felix got an Oscar for its dance direction.

1937 **THE LIFE OF EMILE ZOLA** *(William Dieterle)*
PAUL MUNI, JOSEPH SCHILDKRAUT
A serious dramatic biography this time, which also won story and screenplay Oscars.

1938 **YOU CAN'T TAKE IT WITH YOU** *(Frank Capra)*
LIONEL BARRYMORE, JEAN ARTHUR, JAMES STEWART
Capra also took the director's Oscar for this, the first Academy-Awarded social comedy.

11

Best Picture

1939   **GONE WITH THE WIND** *(Victor Fleming)*
CLARK GABLE, VIVIEN LEIGH, LESLIE HOWARD, OLIVIA de HAVILLAND
One of the most famous successful (and longest) feature films of all time, consistently reissued and still popular decades later.

1940   **REBECCA** *(Alfred Hitchcock)*
LAURENCE OLIVIER, JOAN FONTAINE
An early Hitchcock milestone, adapted from Daphne du Maurier's novel of the same title.

1941   **HOW GREEN WAS MY VALLEY** *(John Ford)*
WALTER PIDGEON, MAUREEN O'HARA, DONALD CRISP
A story of a Welsh miner's family which was richly Oscar-decorated, including one to director Ford, and to Crisp as supporting actor.

1942   **MRS MINIVER** *(William Wyler)*
WALTER PIDGEON, GREER GARSON
A sentimental and artificially quaint story of a middle-class Englishwoman in wartime, which nonetheless won Garson the 'best actress' award.

1943   **CASABLANCA** *(Michael Curtiz)*
HUMPHREY BOGART, INGRID BERGMAN
One of Bogart's best-remembered roles, and a film which has become an archetype of the mid-40s mood.

1944   **GOING MY WAY** *(Leo McCarey)*
BING CROSBY, BARRY FITZGERALD
A much-decorated film (awards for director/writer McCarey and both the principal actors) high on sentimentality.

1945   **THE LOST WEEKEND** *(Billy Wilder)*
RAY MILLAND
Adapted from a novel by Charles Jackson, this also won the screenplay Oscar for co-writers Wilder and Charles Brackett (the producer).

1946   **THE BEST YEARS OF OUR LIVES** *(William Wyler)*
FREDRIC MARCH, MYRNA LOY
Oscars also for March and director Wyler in this then topical, but rapidly dated, drama of 'boys back from the war'.

1947   **GENTLEMAN'S AGREEMENT** *(Elia Kazan)*
GREGORY PECK, DOROTHY McGUIRE
An important early 'conscience' film, indicting the taint of anti-Semitism.

1948   **HAMLET** *(Laurence Olivier)*
LAURENCE OLIVIER, JEAN SIMMONS
The first all-British film (and the only Shakespeare adaptation) to win the 'best picture' Oscar.

1949   **ALL THE KING'S MEN** *(Robert Rossen)*
BRODERICK CRAWFORD
Strong drama of corruption in US State politics from Robert Penn Warren's novel, which had its basis in fact.

1950   **ALL ABOUT EVE** *(Joseph L Mankiewicz)*
ANNE BAXTER, BETTE DAVIS, GEORGE SANDERS
Mankiewicz also won best director and screenplay writer awards for this knife-in-the-back story of the acting profession.

1951   **AN AMERICAN IN PARIS** *(Vincente Minnelli)*
GENE KELLY, LESLIE CARON
The first musical for some years to win the Oscar, and one still favourably remembered and viewed many years on.

1952   **THE GREATEST SHOW ON EARTH** *(Cecil B De Mille)*
JAMES STEWART, CHARLTON HESTON
The only Oscar-winning film by the infamous autocratic master of epic pomp.

1953   **FROM HERE TO ETERNITY** *(Fred Zinnemann)*
BURT LANCASTER, DEBORAH KERR, FRANK SINATRA, DONNA REED
Sinatra and Reed won Oscars for their supporting roles in this famous
melodramatic mixture of love and war.

1954   **ON THE WATERFRONT** *(Elia Kazan)*
MARLON BRANDO, EVA MARIE SAINT
Set in New York's dockland the archetypal early Brando role which earned him
the best actor award.

1955   **MARTY** *(Delbert Mann)*
ERNEST BORGNINE, BETSY BLAIR
Also the winner of the best screenplay award for writer Paddy Chayefsky, who
adapted it from his TV play.

1956   **AROUND THE WORLD IN 80 DAYS** *(Michael Anderson)*
DAVID NIVEN, ROBERT NEWTON
Made in Todd-AO process on a spectacular scale, this adaptation of Jules
Verne's light-hearted adventure had over 40 big names in small cameo roles.

1957   **THE BRIDGE ON THE RIVER KWAI** *(David Lean)*
ALEC GUINNESS, JACK HAWKINS
Set in a Burmese prisoner of war camp, scored a hat-trick with Oscars too for
Guinness and director Lean.

1958   **GIGI** *(Vincente Minnelli)*
LESLIE CARON, MAURICE CHEVALIER, LOUIS JOURDAN
A Lerner & Loewe musical adaptation of Colette's novel, which won nine
Oscars including one for Cecil Beaton's costumes.

1959   **BEN HUR** *(William Wyler)*
CHARLTON HESTON, HUGH GRIFFITH, STEPHEN BOYD
The most Oscar-decorated film of all, with 11 awards including those of director,
actor, and Hugh Griffith as supporting actor.

1960   **THE APARTMENT** *(Billy Wilder)*
JACK LEMMON, SHIRLEY MACLAINE
Wilder won both writer and director awards for this story of a young office clerk
trying to work his way up by nefarious methods.

1961   **WEST SIDE STORY** *(Robert Wise/Jerome Robbins)*
NATALIE WOOD, RICHARD BEYMER, GEORGE CHAKIRIS, RITA
MORENO
Best support Oscars for Chakiris and Moreno in this enduring Leonard
Bernstein-scored musical 20th Century update of 'Romeo and Juliet'.

1962   **LAWRENCE OF ARABIA** *(David Lean)*
PETER O'TOOLE, OMAR SHARIF
David Lean's second Oscar winner and a much awarded film, particularly in the
technical areas.

1963   **TOM JONES** *(Tony Richardson)*
ALBERT FINNEY, EDITH EVANS, HUGH GRIFFITH
Another British film, based on the bawdy Fielding novel of two centuries earlier,
which also won the best director award.

1964   **MY FAIR LADY** *(George Cukor)*
REX HARRISON, AUDREY HEPBURN, STANLEY HOLLOWAY
This was the Lerner/Loewe stage musical of Shaw's 'Pygmalion' transferred to
the screen with most of the original players intact.

1965   **THE SOUND OF MUSIC** *(Robert Wise)*
JULIE ANDREWS, CHRISTOPHER PLUMMER
An even more successful stage musical adaptation, this time by Rodgers and
Hammerstein.

1966   **A MAN FOR ALL SEASONS** *(Fred Zinnemann)*
PAUL SCOFIELD, ROBERT SHAW
This British-made biography of the life of Sir Thomas More also won Scofield the
best actor Oscar for his title role performance.

1967   **IN THE HEAT OF THE NIGHT** *(Norman Jewison)*
ROD STEIGER, SIDNEY POITIER
Ostensibly a murder mystery, this was really all about the antagonistic interplay
of the two lead characters and also earned Steiger an Oscar.

1968   **OLIVER!** *(Carol Reed)*
MARK LESTER, RON MOODY, OLIVER REED
A musical adaptation of Dickens' 'Oliver Twist' which scooped up 6 Oscars,
including the director's award for Reed.

1969   **MIDNIGHT COWBOY** *(John Schlesinger)*
JON VOIGHT, DUSTIN HOFFMAN
Adapted from James Leo Herlihy's novel, this also gained the best screenplay
award for its writer, Waldo Salt.

1970   **PATTON** *(Franklin J Schaffner)*
GEORGE C SCOTT
Notable for winning Scott the best actor Oscar (which he refused), this also
scored for its director and its writers (Francis Ford Coppola and Edmund H
North).

1971   **THE FRENCH CONNECTION** *(William Friedkin)*
GENE HACKMAN, ROY SCHEIDER
A trendsetting gritty treatment of street-level U.S. police work, and another film
which also swept up the best director and actor awards.

1972   **THE GODFATHER** *(Francis Ford Coppola)*
MARLON BRANDO, JAMES CAAN, AL PACINO
The epic film about a Mafia family for which Marlon Brando declined the best
actor award for his title role performance.

Gary Cooper

1973   **THE STING** *(George Roy Hill)*
ROBERT REDFORD, PAUL NEWMAN
An easy-going comedy/drama of the ragtime era which briefly initiated a mini-boom in Scott Joplin's music.

1974   **THE GODFATHER, PART 2** *(Francis Ford Coppola)*
AL PACINO, ROBERT DE NIRO
The only sequel to an Oscar-winning film to be equally honoured; this time, director Coppola got an Oscar as well.

1975   **ONE FLEW OVER THE CUCKOO'S NEST** *(Milos Forman)*
JACK NICHOLSON, LOUISE FLETCHER
Adapted from a novel by Ken Kesey, and another in the very select bunch of films which also gained best director, actor *and* actress awards.

1976   **ROCKY** *(John G Avildsen)*
SYLVESTER STALLONE, TALIA SHIRE, BURGESS MEREDITH
The film which marked Stallone's sudden appearance at the top, though it was Avildsen and his film editors Richard Halsey and Scott Conrad who took the other Oscars here.

1977   **ANNIE HALL** *(Woody Allen)*
WOODY ALLEN, DIANE KEATON
Woody Allen's greatest moment, winning him also the best director and screenplay awards, plus an Oscar for co-star Keaton.

1978   **THE DEER HUNTER** *(Michael Cimino)*
ROBERT DE NIRO, CHRISTOPHER WALKEN
This harrowing post-Vietnam drama also won Cimino the best director award, and another for himself and his three collaborators for its screenplay.

1979   **KRAMER VS KRAMER** *(Robert Benton)*
DUSTIN HOFFMAN, MERYL STREEP
Another board-sweeper, with additional Oscars for Benton (two, as director and as writer of the screenplay), Hoffman and Streep.

1980   **ORDINARY PEOPLE** *(Robert Redford)*
MARY TYLER MOORE, DONALD SUTHERLAND
A triumph for Redford, who proved himself as accomplished a director as he was an actor, and also carried away the appropriate Oscar.

1981   **CHARIOTS OF FIRE** *(Hugh Hudson)*
BEN CROSS, IAN CHARLESON
The British film industry's stunning comeback into Oscar prominence, with additional awards for writer Colin Welland and the music of Vangelis.

A study of this list serves to reinforce the obvious truism that great art and great success do not necessarily go hand-in-hand. Whilst it would be unfair to suggest that any of the Best Picture winners were actually commercial failures, these certainly do not (with odd exceptions) represent the most popular films of all time — as comparison with the list of All-Time Money Makers further on in the book will confirm. The Oscars are, of course, awarded to a picture for its success on a creative level, with little heed of its potential in the commercial marketplace; some of the choices of earlier years may seem a litle quaint to modern critical sensibilities, but then the criteria of creative achievement are subject to change, and the art and craft of movie making have inevitably come of age over the half-century or more under review here. These winners should be remembered and regarded in the context of the era in which they were made — and most of them are indeed a worthwhile viewing experience even now.

Frank Capra

ACADEMY AWARD WINNERS

Best Director

1927/8 **FRANK BORZAGE** *('Seventh Heaven')* and
LEWIS MILESTONE *('Two Arabian Knights')*
Two awards were given in this first year.

1928/9 **FRANK LLOYD** *('The Divine Lady')*
The first of Lloyd's two awards in this category. An ex-actor, he came originally from Scotland.

1929/30 **LEWIS MILESTONE** *('All Quiet On The Western Front')*
Milestone's finest hour, this film also won the best picture Oscar. He failed to gain another, despite making films into the 60s.

1930/1 **NORMAN TAUROG** *('Skippy')*
The only Oscar for Taurog, who ended up in the 60s making Elvis Presley potboilers.

1931/2 **FRANK BORZAGE** *('Bad Girl')*
Borzage's second Oscar was for his first sound film to be so honoured, the earlier 'Seventh Heaven' having been a silent.

1932/3 **FRANK LLOYD** *('Cavalcade')*
The second instance of best picture and director awards for the same production.

1934 **FRANK CAPRA** *('It Happened One Night')*
Capra's first award-winner was also the first 'board-sweeping' film in Oscar history, winning all the major categories.

1935 **JOHN FORD** *('The Informer')*
Ford came from an Irish/American background, which made this drama of revolutionary Dublin an appropriate debut award winner.

1936 **FRANK CAPRA** *('Mr. Deeds Goes To Town')*
A social comedy of the kind which made Capra's reputation through the thirties.

1937 **LEO McCAREY** *('The Awful Truth')*
McCarey also wrote this, the first of his two films to bring him the best director award.

1938 **FRANK CAPRA** *('You Can't Take It With You')*
This zany comedy, which also won the best picture award, completed Capra's hat-trick of 30s Oscars.

1939 **VICTOR FLEMING** *('Gone With The Wind')*
George Cukor got this film underway, but Fleming handled most of its epic length and triumphed.

1940 **JOHN FORD** *('The Grapes Of Wrath')*
From the Steinbeck novel, this film is generally regarded as Ford's best work.

1941 **JOHN FORD** *('How Green Was My Valley')*
A British setting for the film which made Ford the first director to win an Oscar in two successive years.

1942 **WILLIAM WYLER** *('Mrs Miniver')*
The first of three director Oscars for Wyler, with another much-decorated film.

1943   **MICHAEL CURTIZ** *('Casablanca')*
Originally from Hungary, Curtiz made some 40 Hollywood films, mostly action dramas, before this masterpiece gave him his only Oscar.

1944   **LEO McCAREY** *('Going My Way')*
The best (and most award-decorated) example of McCarey's sentimental approach gave him his second Oscar.

1945   **BILLY WILDER** *('The Lost Weekend')*
Another mid-European immigrant, who has made films up to the present day.

1946   **WILLIAM WYLER** *('The Best Years Of Our Lives')*
The second award within four years for this consistent director of German origin.

1947   **ELIA KAZAN** *('Gentleman's Agreement')*
The first of two best director awards for Kazan, whose name came from his Turkish ancestry.

1948   **JOHN HUSTON** *('The Treasure Of Sierre Madre')*
Another actor/director, Huston also wrote this, his only Academy Award winner.

1949   **JOSEPH L MANKIEWICZ** *('A Letter To Three Wives')*
A screenwriter, producer and director, Mankiewicz also wrote (and received an Oscar for) the screenplay here.

1950   **JOSEPH L MANKIEWICZ** *('All About Eve')*
This film made Mankiewicz the second recipient of a best director award in consecutive years. Uniquely, he also won the screenplay Oscar for the second year running.

1951   **GEORGE STEVENS** *('A Place In The Sun')*
The first of two director awards for Stevens, who had been making films since the early 30s.

1952   **JOHN FORD** *('The Quiet Man')*
Another Irish background for Ford's fourth award-winner, a romantic comedy with John Wayne.

1953   **FRED ZINNEMANN** *('From Here To Eternity')*
The first of two best director awards for Zinnemann, who came to Hollywood from Austria in the 20s.

1954   **ELIA KAZAN** *('On The Waterfront')*
Kazan's second win, during his most artistically and commercially successful period — which also produced 'A Streetcar Named Desire', 'East Of Eden' and 'Baby Doll'.

1955   **DELBERT MANN** *('Marty')*
Amazingly, this was Mann's first major feature film; he had come from TV direction, and after a solid big-screen run through the 50s and 60s, eventually went almost full circle by returning to making T.V. movies.

1956   **GEORGE STEVENS** *('Giant')*
Stevens' second award-winner highlighted James Dean, an actor whose promise was extinguished by his premature death.

1957   **DAVID LEAN** *('The Bridge On The River Kwai')*
Lean was the first British director of a British film to win this award, with a production which also scooped best picture.

1958   **VINCENTE MINNELLI** *('Gigi')*
Minnelli had previously directed 'An American In Paris', which won a best picture award, but 'Gigi' gave him his only director's Oscar.

1959   **WILLIAM WYLER** *('Ben Hur')*
Wyler's spectacular tour de force has received more Oscar awards than any other film.

1960   **BILLY WILDER** *('The Apartment')*
Wilder's second best director award, 15 years after the first, the film also won him a best writer Oscar.

William Wyler

Mike Nichols

1961   JEROME ROBBINS & ROBERT WISE *('West Side Story')*
The only such award for this partnership; Robbins was basically the choreographer/director of the dance sequences.

1962   DAVID LEAN *('Lawrence Of Arabia')*
The second award for Lean in this category; strangely, he has made few major films since this.

1963   TONY RICHARDSON *('Tom Jones')*
The only Oscar for Richardson made him the second Briton to win this category in successive years. He showed here the fulfillment of the promise evident in, for instance, 'A Taste Of Honey' and 'The Loneliness Of The Long Distance Runner'.

1964   GEORGE CUKOR *('My Fair Lady')*
Cukor's only award for best director, though he had a career of distinguished films running back to the early 30s.

1965   ROBERT WISE *('The Sound Of Music')*
Though most of Wise's films have been dramas, this was his second musical to earn him an Oscar.

1966   FRED ZINNEMANN *('A Man For All Seasons')*
Zinnemann's second award, this time with a British cast, crew and location. He constructed a strong historical film with no resort to any of the epic clichés.

1967   MIKE NICHOLS *('The Graduate')*
Born Michael Peschkowsky in Germany, Nichols directed a small number of well-remembered films, of which this was the best.

1968   CAROL REED *('Oliver!')*
This was a late revival for Sir Carol Reed, most of whose films had been made during the 30s and 40s.

1969   JOHN SCHLESINGER *('Midnight Cowboy')*
This was Englishman Schlesinger's first American film, again built on a strong British reputation from 'Billy Liar', 'A Kind Of Loving' and 'Darling'.

1970   FRANKLIN J SCHAFFNER *('Patton')*
Another director of a comparatively small but well-remembered canon of films (others include 'Planet Of The Apes' and 'Nicholas and Alexandra').

1971   WILLIAM FRIEDKIN *('The French Connection')*
Freidkin's only directorial award-winner also scooped the best picture category. He moved on next to make 'The Exorcist'.

1972   BOB FOSSE *('Cabaret')*
Originally a dancer, Fosse generally both directed and choreographed his films, as he did here.

1973   GEORGE ROY HILL *('The Sting')*
Hill had previously made 'Butch Cassidy and the Sundance Kid' with Newman and Redford; this film with the same team proved his triumph.

1974   FRANCIS FORD COPPOLA *('The Godfather, Part 2')*
Coppola had, of course, directed Part 1 as well, which had taken the best picture award in 1972. He thus achieved a unique double with this sequel.

1975   MILOS FORMAN *('One Flew Over The Cuckoo's Nest')*
A Czechoslovakian director this was Forman's debut in America and this drama received several awards.

1976   JOHN G AVILDSEN *('Rocky')*
Avildsen had made some eight lesser films through the decade prior to this, but 'Rocky' is by far his most successful work.

1977   WOODY ALLEN *('Annie Hall')*
Born Allen Konigsberg, this well-known comedian wrote, directed and starred in several cult-favourite films, before this one finally swept most of the year's major Oscars.

1978   MICHAEL CIMINO *('The Deer Hunter')*
Cimino began as a screenplay writer (his credits include Clint Eastwood's 'Magnum Force'), and this was only his second major film as director.

1979   **ROBERT BENTON** *('Kramer Vs. Kramer')*
This film gained several awards; Benton also wrote the screenplay, and won an
Oscar for that too.

1980   **ROBERT REDFORD** *('Ordinary People')*
Redford had achieved the peak of his acting profession when he turned to
direction — with equal flair and success.

1981   **WARREN BEATTY** *('Reds')*
Another accomplished actor-turned-director, Beatty gained the Oscar here that
he had never managed to win as a performer.

Through more than 50 years of film making, there have obviously been more
fine movie directors than there were Academy Awards to honour their craft —
and this, when it comes down to it, is the only real reason why so many film
makers whose work is regarded as a milestone in cinema history are only
represented once on this list, or not at all. In the early years, for instance, the
Best Director award was only presented to an American, because the awards
were considered to be for the achievements of the American Film Industry. This
parochial attitude eventually disappeared as the industry became international in
scope, but for this reason most of the great European directors of the last 50
years were never even considered for nomination here, let alone awarded.

That said, the fact that there was only ever one award to be won at any given
time does say much for the enduring talents of those men whose names appear
on the listing more than once. While nobody would be foolish enough to argue
that John Ford should be considered a better director than Alfred Hitchcock or
Stanley Kubrick simply because Ford won four Oscars and the other two names
do not appear at all, it is certainly a salute to consistency of craft.

Alec Guinness, Sam Spiegel, Jack Hawkins, David Lean

21

Humphrey Bogart

ACADEMY AWARD WINNERS

Best Actor

1927/8 **EMIL JANNINGS** (in *'The Last Command'* and *'The Way Of All Flesh'*)
Jannings — whose real name was Theodor Emil Janenz — was a German actor who came to silent films from the stage.

1928/9 **WARNER BAXTER** (in *'Old Arizona'*)
Baxter made his first silent in 1914, and survived into the talkie era with regular films until his death in 1951.

1929/30 **GEORGE ARLISS** (in *'Disraeli'*)
A veteran British stage actor, Arliss found a new lease of life on the screen throughout the 30s.

1930/1 **LIONEL BARRYMORE** (in *'A Free Soul'*)
The only best actor Oscar for the Barrymore brothers. Lionel filmed almost solidly from 1909 until his death in 1954.

1931/2 **FREDRIC MARCH** (in *'Dr. Jekyll and Mr. Hyde'*) and
WALLACE BEERY (in *'The Champ'*)
This is the only instance to date of a tie for this award. A consistent career through the 30s, however, failed to bring a follow-up to Wallace Beery.

1932/3 **CHARLES LAUGHTON** (in *'The Private Life Of Henry VIII'*)
Laughton's success made him the first British actor in a British-made film to win this award.

1934 **CLARK GABLE** (in *'It Happened One Night'*)
Gable's only best actor Oscar, despite his plethora of other hugely successful lead roles.

1935 **VICTOR McLAGLEN** (in *'The Informer'*)
A British silent star who went to Hollywood during the 20s and then filmed consistently until the late 50s.

1936 **PAUL MUNI** (in *'The Story Of Louis Pasteur'*)
Born Muni Weisenfreund, Muni moved from stage to screen in the early 30s, this film bringing his only Oscar.

1937 **SPENCER TRACY** (in *'Captains Courageous'*)
Tracy become one of the most respected of Hollywood actors through over three decades on the screen, and this Kipling story brought him his first major award.

1938 **SPENCER TRACY** (in *'Boys Town'*)
With this role, Tracy became the first actor (and to date, the only one) to win the Oscar in consecutive years.

1939 **ROBERT DONAT** (in *'Goodbye Mr Chips'*)
The only Oscar for this consistently popular British actor of the 30s and 40s.

1940 **JAMES STEWART** (in *'The Philadelphia Story'*)
Consistently on screen in romantic and comedy roles from 1935 to date, this was also Stewart's only Oscar-winning performance.

1941 **GARY COOPER** (in *'Sergeant York'*)
The first of two awards for Cooper, who enjoyed more than three decades of strong and popular lead roles.

1942 **JAMES CAGNEY** (in *'Yankee Doodle Dandy'*)
Cagney's only Oscar was not for a tough guy role, but for his best-remembered singing, dancing part.

1943 **PAUL LUKAS** (in *'Watch On The Rhine'*)
Originally from Hungary, Lukas had a Hollywood career which spanned some 40 years.

1944 **BING CROSBY** (in *'Going My Way'*)
A box office and recording star of considerable longevity, Crosby found one of his most enduring screen images in this singing priest role.

1945 **RAY MILLAND** (in *'The Lost Weekend'*)
Another British expatriot to Hollywood, Milland has filmed consistently from 1929 to the present day, occasionally brilliantly, as here.

1946 **FREDRIC MARCH** (in *'The Best Years Of Our Lives'*)
March, whose real name was Frederick Bickel, was notable for the consummate quality of his many performances; this was his second Oscar, won 14 years after the first.

1947 **RONALD COLMAN** (in *'A Double Life'*)
A British-born Hollywood actor who became well-loved in his many romantic adventurer roles, Colman gained his only Oscar here.

1948 **LAURENCE OLIVIER** (in *'Hamlet'*)
Appropriately, one of Britain's greatest classic actors gained his Academy Award in a Shakespearean role.

1949 **BRODERICK CRAWFORD** (in *'All The King's Men'*)
A heavyweight actor best known for his cops and/or robbers roles, Crawford later became even more of a household name in his 'Highway Patrol' TV series.

Jack Lemmon

Richard Burton

John Wayne

Humphrey Bogart

1950   **JOSE FERRER** (in *'Cyrano de Bergerac'*)
Real name Jose Vincente Ferrer y Centron, he had a respected stage career
before belatedly taking to the screen (and not leaving it to date.)

1951   **HUMPHREY BOGART** (in *'The African Queen'*)
Like so many of his distinguished contemporaries, Bogart received only one
Oscar, for this typically gritty role as a riverboat captain.

1952   **GARY COOPER** (in *'High Noon'*)
Cooper's second Oscar was for a superb role which established a classic
archetype of the reluctant Western hero.

1953   **WILLIAM HOLDEN** (in *'Stalag 17'*)
Consistently popular in action hero roles and later more distinguished parts for
some four decades until his recent death, Holden won his only best actor award
for this dramatic war role.

1954   **MARLON BRANDO** (in *'On The Waterfront'*)
One of the best-remembered images of the early, smouldering tough guy
Brando, and the first of two best actor awards.

1955   **ERNEST BORGNINE** (in *'Marty'*)
A gritty character actor of wide versatility, Borgnine has worked on screen
successfully up to the present day. This was his only Oscar.

1956   **YUL BRYNNER** (in *'The King And I'*)
This famous bald actor was awarded an Oscar for one of his best-remembered
but nonetheless least characteristic roles.

1957   **ALEC GUINNESS** (in *'The Bridge On The River Kwai'*)
One of the most respected and versatile of all British actors, Guinness'
performance added to the multitude of award triumphs for this film.

1958   **DAVID NIVEN** (in *'Separate Tables'*)
Master of the debonair British image on the screen from the mid 30s until the
present day, Niven also received just one Academy Award, as best actor.

1959   **CHARLTON HESTON** (in *'Ben Hur'*)
Heston became renowned for his dominating lead roles in huge historical and
Biblical epics; this was undoubtedly the best.

1960   **BURT LANCASTER** (in *'Elmer Gantry'*)
Another hugely versatile actor whose popularity on screen endures to the
present day, although he has won this award only once.

1961   **MAXIMILIAN SCHELL** (in *'Judgment at Nuremberg'*)
An Austrian, Schell soon became a familiar face in international films: this one
was an early milestone for him.

1962   **GREGORY PECK** (in *'To Kill a Mockingbird'*)
Another master of action-adventure and latterly more distinguished lead roles,
Peck is another of Hollywood's grand masters to have received an Oscar only
once.

1963   **SIDNEY POITIER** (in *'Lilies of the Field'*)
The first black actor to gain international fame and respect on a lasting basis, he
gave one of his most sensitive performances in this film.

1964   **REX HARRISON** (in *'My Fair Lady'*)
A veteran of both stage and screen, Harrison fitted his old stage role in this film
so comfortably that he almost seemed to be playing himself.

1965   **LEE MARVIN** (in *'Cat Ballou'*)
Best-known for his tough guy and villainous roles, it is ironic that Marvin
received his Oscar for this idiosyncratic performance as a permanently drunken
cowboy.

1966   **PAUL SCOFIELD** (in *'A Man For All Seasons'*)
A distinguished British classical actor with long stage experience, Scofield found
by far his most rewarding film role here.

1967   **ROD STEIGER** (in *'In the Heat of the Night'*)
Another dynamic character actor of wide ability, who found his strongest roles
here and in 'The Pawnbroker'.

1968   **CLIFF ROBERTSON** (in *'Charly'*)
This challenging role as a man who evolved from a simpleton to a genius and
back again gave this consistently popular lead actor his only Oscar.

1969   **JOHN WAYNE** (in *'True Grit'*)
After decades of huge box office success as the screen's greatest tough guy hero,
Wayne finally got his Oscar for this grittily eccentric Western role.

1970   **GEORGE C SCOTT** (in *'Patton'*)
Scott made history by being the first actor to refuse to accept the Academy
Award, for his role as an American Second World War tank hero.

Marlon Brando

1971 **GENE HACKMAN** (in 'The French Connection')
After ten years on the screen, this film brought sudden fame to Hackman, who went on to become one of the biggest stars of the 70s.

1972 **MARLON BRANDO** (in 'The Godfather')
Brando followed George C Scott's lead and declined his award, using the ceremony instead to make a statement about Red Indian emancipation.

1973 **JACK LEMMON** (in 'Save The Tiger')
Lemmon's only best actor Oscar, following many years of successful and sophisticated comedy roles.

1974 **ART CARNEY** (in 'Harry And Tonto')
Better known as a TV comedy actor, Carney has made comparatively few films, and his is probably the least familiar name at this end of the list.

1975 **JACK NICHOLSON** (in 'One Flew Over the Cuckoo's Nest')
This black comedy role suited Nicholson's oddly menacing style, which had already made him a top box office name.

1976 **PETER FINCH** (in 'Network')
His celebrated role as a newsreader on American TV was one which stretched Finch's tremendous talents to the full, although it totally dominated this biting film. It also proved to be his final role.

1977 **RICHARD DREYFUSS** (in 'The Goodbye Girl')
Another actor who had rapidly become a top box office attraction by the end of the 70s, Dreyfuss showed his talent as a first-rate comedic actor.

1978 **JON VOIGHT** (in 'Coming Home')
A taxing part as a veteran returned from Vietnam showed a considerably more mature Voight than the one who had first been noticed a few years earlier in 'Midnight Cowboy'.

1979 **DUSTIN HOFFMAN** (in 'Kramer Vs. Kramer')
Having taken more youthful roles in his earlier successes, this film had Hoffman in a solidly parental role, as a man desperately trying to hold on to his child in a hopelessly divided marriage.

1980 **ROBERT DE NIRO** (in 'Raging Bull')
De Niro is at times hardly recognisable, so much did he throw himself into this physically demanding part — clearly his best role yet.

1981 **HENRY FONDA** (in 'On Golden Pond')
This sensitive study of crotchetty old age by Fonda was, as usual, seemingly effortless and played with consummate attention to detail.

As with films, it is not necessarily the case that the best actors make the best commercial success. There are many names which do not appear amongst the honours who are widely regarded, and whose box office figures confirm them, as some of the most popular screen actors of all time — names like Clint Eastwood, Steve McQueen, Richard Burton, Paul Newman, Robert Redford and Burt Reynolds, to mention some from the more recent movie years. They do not appear simply because the Best Actor award is given only for the quality of a performance in a given role — and regardless of how much quality comes up for nomination in any given year, there is still only one award. Some of those mentioned above have, in fact, been nominated for Oscars in the past; others, it might be considered, have a style and image which attracts audiences to their films, while lacking the acting talent to gain an award. Few of the performance categories in the Academy awards are marked by multiple winners, and this is perhaps particularly the case with the Best Actor section, where Spencer Tracy, Fredric March, Gary Cooper and Marlon Brando are the only names which appear on two occasions.

Charles Farrell, Janet Gaynor

ACADEMY AWARD WINNERS

Best Actress

1927/8 **JANET GAYNOR** (in *'Seventh Heaven'*, *'Street Angel'* and *'Sunrise'*)
A familiar star of romantic and sentimental silents, who moved into sound films in the 30s.

1928/9 **MARY PICKFORD** (in *'Coquette'*)
Pickford — a Canadian — was probably the most popular and successful female star of the silents, who made her first film in 1909.

1929/30 **NORMA SHEARER** (in *'The Divorcee'*)
Another consistent leading lady, Shearer filmed in silents from 1920 and in talkies until the early 40s.

1930/1 **MARIE DRESSLER** (in *'Min and Bill'*)
Marie Dressler (her real name was Leila Von Koerber) was hugely popular in middle-aged, comedy roles through the 20s and 30s.

1931/2 **HELEN HAYES** (in *'The Sin of Madelon Claudet'*)
A highly-rated stage actress who has filmed occasionally, from the 30s to date, latterly in 'elderly' comic and dramatic roles.

1932/3 **KATHARINE HEPBURN** (in *'Morning Glory'*)
A zestful first award winning performance by Hepburn, as an actress whose talent and wilful character in combination tended to cause problems for those around her.

1934 **CLAUDETTE COLBERT** (in *'It Happened One Night'*)
This film received several awards and brought Colbert, an original champion of 'emancipated woman' roles, her only Oscar.

1935 **BETTE DAVIS** (in *'Dangerous'*)
A typically intense role for Davis, during her most prolific period which had already seen her in almost 30 films in the four years prior to this.

1936 **LUISE RAINER** (in *'The Great Ziegfeld'*)
Originally from Austria, Rainer was another stage actress who appeared only occasionally in films.

1937 **LUISE RAINER** (in *'The Good Earth'*)
With this role, Luise Rainer became the first actress to win two Oscars, and the first of only two (Katharine Hepburn being the other) to gain them in successive years.

1938 **BETTE DAVIS** (in *'Jezebel'*)
This gave Davis her second win, and surprisingly her last, despite a career lasting until the present day in increasingly off-beat dramatic roles.

1939 **VIVIEN LEIGH** (in *'Gone With The Wind'*)
The first British best actress Oscar recipient, for what is still her best-remembered role, in this most enduring of films.

1940 **GINGER ROGERS** (in *'Kitty Foyle'*)
Real name Virginia McMath, Ginger is probably Hollywood's best-remembered dancing/singing leading lady, immortalised by her partnership with Fred Astaire.

1941 **JOAN FONTAINE** (in *'Suspicion'*)
The second Briton (though born in Japan!) to take this award, playing an unusual role in a Hitchcock drama which had her as the potential murder victim of film husband Cary Grant.

Best Actress

Irving Thalberg, Bette Davis, Frank Capra, Victor McLaglen

1942 **GREER GARSON** (in *'Mrs Miniver'*)
An over-sentimentalised role as a British middle-class wife adapting and reacting to the changes which the war was making on the people and country around her, captivated American audiences despite its inherent artificiality.

1943 **JENNIFER JONES** (in *'The Song Of Bernadette'*)
The only award for this actress who made many familiar films through the 40s and 50s, and reappeared in 'The Towering Inferno' in 1974.

1944 **INGRID BERGMAN** (in *'Gaslight'*)
A Swedish actress who found world reknown in the USA and has filmed consistently to the present day. This was the first of two awards.

1945 **JOAN CRAWFORD** (in *'Mildred Pierce'*)
One of Hollywood's best-known and most prolific dramatic actresses, Crawford worked solidly through to the end of the 60s.

1946 **OLIVIA DE HAVILLAND** (in *'To Each His Own'*)
Sister of Joan Fontaine, and another enduring talent who moved steadily from light roles to serious dramatic parts as she matured.

1947 **LORETTA YOUNG** (in *'The Farmer's Daughter'*)
A popular leading lady for some 30 years, this comedy role gave Loretta Young her only Oscar.

1948 **JANE WYMAN** (in *'Johnny Belinda'*)
A popular light and dramatic actress through the 40s and early 50s.

1949 **OLIVIA DE HAVILLAND** (in *'The Heiress'*)
The second win for Olivia within four years, in a film adapted from Henry James' 'Washington Square'.

Mary Astor

1950   **JUDY HOLLIDAY** (in *'Born Yesterday'*)
A popular comedy actress who made comparatively few films, mainly in the early 50s.

1951   **VIVIEN LEIGH** (in *'A Streetcar Named Desire'*)
The second Oscar for Leigh, in this strong dramatic role opposite Marlon Brando.

1952   **SHIRLEY BOOTH** (in *'Come Back Little Sheba'*)
Another of America's highly respected stage actresses, who came late to a small number of films.

1953   **AUDREY HEPBURN** (in *'Roman Holiday'*)
The only Oscar for Hepburn, in one of the lighter roles which preceded better remembered appearances in 'The Nun's Story', 'Breakfast At Tiffany's' and 'Charade'.

1954   **GRACE KELLY** (in *'The Country Girl'*)
Also the only Oscar for this popular actress in light roles, who went on to become Princess Grace of Monaco.

1955   **ANNA MAGNANI** (in *'The Rose Tattoo'*)
The first Italian recipient of this award, seen throughout most of her career in European films.

1956   **INGRID BERGMAN** (in *'Anastasia'*)
This was Bergman's first Hollywood role after a long absence in Europe; she was interestingly cast as the woman claiming to be the daughter of the last Czar of Russia who was believed to have been executed.

1957   **JOANNE WOODWARD** (in *'The Three Faces Of Eve'*)
A consistent light and dramatic actress from the mid 50s to date, married to Paul Newman, and the only best performer Oscar holder in the family!

1958   **SUSAN HAYWARD** (in *'I Want To Live'*)
Real name Edythe Marrener, Hayward specialised in strong and forceful female roles, usually in action films or epics.

1959   **SIMONE SIGNORET** (in *'Room At The Top'*)
This marked a combination unique at the time: an accomplished French actress honoured for a role in a British film.

1960   **ELIZABETH TAYLOR** (in *'Butterfield 8'*)
Taylor began her successful box office career as a child star, though this somewhat controversial role was the culmination of a run of strong adult parts in 'Giant', 'Cat On A Hot Tin Roof' and 'Suddenly Last Summer'.

1961   **SOPHIA LOREN** (in *'Two Women'*)
Italy's second female Oscar winner, in an Italian film by Vittorio De Sica.

1962   **ANNE BANCROFT** (in *'The Miracle Worker'*)
This heralded the third and most successful stage of Bancroft's career, after a run of low-grade 50s films and a therapeutic exile to the Broadway stage. Similar strong parts followed in 'The Pumpkin Eater' and 'The Slender Thread'.

1963   **PATRICIA NEAL** (in *'Hud'*)
A popular leading lady for some 30 years, from the early 50s to date. This role opposite Paul Newman brought her only Oscar.

1964   **JULIE ANDREWS** (in *'Mary Poppins'*)
One of Britain's most spectacularly successful actresses at the box office; this Disney musical role exemplified her lighter side.

1965   **JULIE CHRISTIE** (in *'Darling'*)
Another one time British winner, for a strong early role in a British film opposite Dirk Bogarde.

1966   **ELIZABETH TAYLOR** (in *'Who's Afraid Of Virginia Woolf?'*)
Taylor's second award, in this much-honoured film, opposite her then-husband Richard Burton.

1967   **KATHARINE HEPBURN** (in *'Guess Who's Coming To Dinner'*)
Hepburn's second award after 35 years, for the last of her classic screen partnerships with Spencer Tracy.

Julie Andrews

Glenda Jackson

Barbara Streisand

1968   **KATHARINE HEPBURN** (in *'The Lion In Winter'*) and
BARBRA STREISAND (in *'Funny Girl'*)
The single instance ever of a tie for this award. This was Streisand's only Oscar to date, and Hepburn's third — the second in successive years — making her only the second actress to achieve this latter feat.

1969   **MAGGIE SMITH** (in *'The Prime of Miss Jean Brodie'*)
This brilliantly observed portrayal of a professed liberal and liberated (but in fact hopelessly misled) schoolteacher of the between-war years brought another well-earned British Oscar.

1970   **GLENDA JACKSON** (in *'Women In Love'*)
The second consecutive British winner, and the first for Glenda Jackson for her powerful role in this D.H. Lawrence adaptation.

1971   **JANE FONDA** (in *'Klute'*)
The first of the Fondas to win an Oscar, Jane eschewed the glamorous roles of her previous films to play the cool-headed, warm-hearted prostitute in this gritty street-level story.

1972   **LIZA MINNELLI** (in *'Cabaret'*)
Liza's powerful acting, singing and dancing in this much-honoured musical gave Judy Garland's daughter her only Oscar to date.

1973   **GLENDA JACKSON** (in *'A Touch of Class'*)
The second award for Glenda, this time in a sophisticated comedy role opposite George Segal.

1974   **ELLEN BURSTYN** (in *'Alice Doesn't Live Here Anymore'*)
Ellen's widely awarded role here followed a handful of little-remembered 60s films and then stronger parts in 'The Last Picture Show' and 'The Exorcist'. Strangely, she has hardly been seen on the screen since.

1975   **LOUISE FLETCHER** (in *'One Flew Over The Cuckoo's Nest'*)
In middle age, and after only a couple of previous films, Louise received multiple awards for her role in this most-decorated film of the mid 70s.

1976 **FAYE DUNAWAY** (in *'Network'*)
A major box office attraction through the 70s, Faye Dunaway took her only Oscar together with co-star Peter Finch in this bitter satire on TV.

1977 **DIANE KEATON** (in *'Annie Hall'*)
Woody Allen's protégée Keaton received her only Oscar to date in this most-honoured of Allen's highly personalised films.

1978 **JANE FONDA** (in *'Coming Home'*)
Another strong dramatic role brought Jane's second Oscar, together with an award for co-star Jon Voight.

1979 **SALLY FIELD** (in *'Norma Rae'*)
Sally Field emerged from several years in TV series and two films ('Hooper' and 'Smokey And The Bandit') opposite Burt Reynolds before securing this strong title role.

1980 **SISSY SPACEK** (in *'Coal Miner's Daughter'*)
Another comparative newcomer with few previous major lead roles, Sissy Spacek won the award for her portrayal of singer Loretta Lynn in this biographical film.

1981 **KATHARINE HEPBURN** (in *'On Golden Pond'*)
Hepburn's fourth win (an Academy record in this category), paired her with Henry Fonda in husband-and-wife roles, allowing full scope to both her emotional range and her talent for comedy.

Interestingly, female performers seem to be more consistently awarded by their Hollywood peers than their male counterparts. It is probably true to say that there are few actresses who readily spring to mind as major movie attractions over the last 50 years or so, who are not actually represented somewhere on this list. Perhaps competition isn't so fierce, though doubtless the acting profession would hotly dispute that. Certainly Katharine Hepburn's four wins are unlikely ever to be equalled by an actor — and her period of Oscar success stretching from 1933 to 1981 will probably never be matched for consistency and longevity by anyone.

John Mills

ACADEMY AWARD WINNERS

Best Supporting Actor

This award was first made in 1936, and since then has been a continuous feature of the Oscar ceremony. Of the 'Best Supporting Actor' recipients, just two, Jack Lemmon and Robert De Niro, have also gone on to win the 'Best Actor' award.

1936	**WALTER BRENNAN** (in *'Come And Get It!'*)
1937	**JOSEPH SCHILDKRAUT** (in *'The Life Of Emile Zola'*)
1938	**WALTER BRENNAN** (in *'Kentucky'*)
1939	**THOMAS MITCHELL** (in *'Stagecoach'*)
1940	**WALTER BRENNAN** (in *'The Westerner'*)
1941	**DONALD CRISP** (in *'How Green Was My Valley'*)
1942	**VAN HEFLIN** (in *'Johnny Eager'*)
1943	**CHARLES COBURN** (in *'The More the Merrier'*)
1944	**BARRY FITZGERALD** (in *'Going My Way'*)
1945	**JAMES DUNN** (in *'A Tree Grows in Brooklyn'*)
1946	**HAROLD RUSSELL** (in *'The Best Years of Our Lives'*)
1947	**EDMUND GWENN** (in *'Miracle on 34th Street'*)
1948	**WALTER HUDSON** (in *'The Treasure of the Sierra Madre'*)
1949	**DEAN JAGGER** (in *'Twelve O'Clock High'*)
1950	**GEORGE SANDERS** (in *'All About Eve'*)
1951	**KARL MALDEN** (in *'A Streetcar Named Desire'*)
1952	**ANTHONY QUINN** (in *'Viva Zapata!'*)
1953	**FRANK SINATRA** (in *'From Here To Eternity'*)
1954	**EDMOND O'BRIEN** (in *'The Barefoot Contessa'*)
1955	**JACK LEMMON** (in *'Mister Roberts'*)
1956	**ANTHONY QUINN** (in *'Lust For Life'*)
1957	**RED BUTTONS** (in *'Sayonara'*)
1958	**BURL IVES** (in *'The Big Country'*)
1959	**HUGH GRIFFITH** (in *'Ben Hur'*)
1960	**PETER USTINOV** (in *'Spartacus'*)
1961	**GEORGE CHAKIRIS** (in *'West Side Story'*)
1962	**ED BEGLEY** (in *'Sweet Bird of Youth'*)
1963	**MELVYN DOUGLAS** (in *'Hud'*)
1964	**PETER USTINOV** (in *'Topkapi'*)
1965	**MARTIN BALSAM** (in *'A Thousand Clowns'*)
1966	**WALTER MATTHAU** (in *'The Fortune Cookie'* — retitled *'Meet Whiplash Willie'* in Britain)
1967	**GEORGE KENNEDY** (in *'Cool Hand Luke'*)
1968	**JACK ALBERTSON** (in *'The Subject was Roses'*)

Donald Crisp

1969	**GIG YOUNG** (in *'They Shoot Horses, Don't They?'*)
1970	**JOHN MILLS** (in *'Ryan's Daughter'*)
1971	**BEN JOHNSON** (in *'The Last Picture Show'*)
1972	**JOEL GREY** (in *'Cabaret'*)
1973	**JOHN HOUSEMAN** (in *'The Paper Chase'*)
1974	**ROBERT DE NIRO** (in *'The Godfather, Part II'*)
1975	**GEORGE BURNS** (in *'The Sunshine Boys'*)
1976	**JASON ROBARDS** (in *'All the President's Men'*)
1977	**JASON ROBARDS** (in *'Julia'*)
1978	**CHRISTOPHER WALKEN** (in *'The Deer Hunter'*)
1979	**MELVYN DOUGLAS** (in *'Being There'*)
1980	**TIMOTHY HUTTON** (in *'Ordinary People'*)
1981	**JOHN GIELGUD** (in *'Arthur'*)

One interesting point demonstrated by the names on this list, and perhaps not too surprising in view of the nature of many supporting roles, is the comparative maturity of many of the actors at the time of their win. More often than not, it seems, the best supporting actor in a film is older than the lead player he is supporting! This has served, if nothing else, to bring academy recognition (in many cases belated) to many seasoned performers in their mature years.

Margaret Rutherford

42

ACADEMY AWARD WINNERS

Best Supporting Actress

This award, like its male counterpart, was inaugurated in 1936, and has continued to be presented since that date. Ingrid Bergman, Helen Hayes and Maggie Smith are the only performers to have won this and the best actress award, although in all three cases the Oscar for supporting actress was won at a later date — nine years on in Miss Smith's case, 30 years in Miss Bergman's and 39 years in Miss Hayes'.

1936	**GALE SONDERGAARD** (in *'Anthony Adverse'*)
1937	**ALICE BRADY** (in *'In Old Chicago'*)
1938	**FAY BAINTER** (in *'Jezebel'*)
1939	**HATTIE McDANIEL** (in *'Gone with the Wind'*)
1940	**JANE DARWELL** (in *'The Grapes of Wrath'*)
1941	**MARY ASTOR** (in *'The Great Lie'*)
1942	**TERESA WRIGHT** (in *'Mrs Miniver'*)
1943	**KATINA PAXINOU** (in *'For Whom the Bell Tolls'*)
1944	**ETHEL BARRYMORE** (in *'None but the Lonely Heart'*)
1945	**ANNE REVERE** (in *'National Velvet'*)
1946	**ANNE BAXTER** (in *'The Razor's Edge'*)
1947	**CELESTE HOLM** (in *'Gentleman's Agreement'*)
1948	**CLAIRE TREVOR** (in *'Key Largo'*)
1949	**MERCEDES McCAMBRIDGE** (in *'All the King's Men'*)
1950	**JOSEPHINE HULL** (in *'Harvey'*)
1951	**KIM HUNTER** (in *'A Streetcar Named Desire'*)
1952	**GLORIA GRAHAME** (in *'The Bad and the Beautiful'*)
1953	**DONNA REED** (in *'From Here to Eternity'*)
1954	**EVA MARIE SAINT** (in *'On the Waterfront'*)
1955	**JO VAN FLEET** (in *'East of Eden'*)
1956	**DOROTHY MALONE** (in *'Written on the Wind'*)
1957	**MIYOSHI UMEKI** (in *'Sayonara'*)
1958	**WENDY HILLER** (in *'Separate Tables'*)
1959	**SHELLEY WINTERS** (in *'The Diary of Anne Frank'*)
1960	**SHIRLEY JONES** (in *'Elmer Gantry'*)
1961	**RITA MORENO** (in *'West Side Story'*)
1962	**PATTY DUKE** (in *'The Miracle Worker'*)
1963	**MARGARET RUTHERFORD** (in *'The VIPs'*)
1964	**LILA KEDROVA** (in *'Zorba the Greek'*)
1965	**SHELLEY WINTERS** (in *'A Patch of Blue'*)
1966	**SANDY DENNIS** (in *'Who's Afraid of Virginia Woolf?'*)
1967	**ESTELLE PARSONS** (in *'Bonnie and Clyde'*)
1968	**RUTH GORDON** (in *'Rosemary's Baby'*)

Maggie Smith

44

1969	**GOLDIE HAWN** (in *'Cactus Flower'*)
1970	**HELEN HAYES** (in *'Airport'*)
1971	**CLORIS LEACHMAN** (in *'The Last Picture Show'*)
1972	**EILEEN HECKART** (in *'Butterflies are Free'*)
1973	**TATUM O'NEAL** (in *'Paper Moon'*)
1974	**INGRID BERGMAN** (in *'Murder on the Orient Express'*)
1975	**LEE GRANT** (in *'Shampoo'*)
1976	**BEATRICE STRAIGHT** (in *'Network'*)
1977	**VANESSA REDGRAVE** (in *'Julia'*)
1978	**MAGGIE SMITH** (in *'California Suite'*)
1979	**MERYL STREEP** (in *'Kramer Vs. Kramer'*)
1980	**MARY STEENBURGEN** (in *'Melvin and Howard'*)
1981	**MAUREEN STAPLETON** (in *'Reds'*)

For no apparent reason , this listing shows a wider age spread than its male equivalent, with less emphasis on mature performers (although there are veterans here of the calibre of Margaret Rutherford, Helen Hayes and Ingrid Bergman). There are also fewer instances of repeated awards — Shelley Winters, in fact, stands alone as the recipient of two best supporting actress awards.

Jacques Tati

ACADEMY AWARD WINNERS

Best Foreign Language Film

From 1947, under the Academy's Special Awards category, a foreign language film of exceptional merit was normally cited (an exception being in 1953). In the 1956 Awards Ceremony, this was organised into a specific foreign language film category which has remained, and arguably grown in importance, through subsequent years. The listings show the title of each film, the director (bracketed) and the country of origin.

1947   **SHOE SHINE** *(Vittoria De Sica)* from Italy
1948   **MONSIEUR VINCENT** *(Maurice Cloche)* from France
1949   **THE BICYCLE THIEVES** (Vittorio De Sica) from Italy
1950   **THE WALLS OF MALAPAGA** *(René Clément)* French/Italian co-production
1951   **RASHOMON** *(Akira Kurosawa)* from Japan
1952   **JEUX INTERDITS** *(Rene Clément) from France*
1953   **(NO AWARD GIVEN)**
1954   **JIGOKUMON (GATE OF HELL)** *(Teinosuke Kinugasa)* from Japan
1955   **SEVEN SAMURAI** *(Akira Kurosawa)* from Japan
1956   **LA STRADA** *(Federico Fellini)* from Italy
1957   **THE NIGHTS OF CABIRIA** *(Federico Fillini)* from Italy
1958   **MON ONCLE** *(Jacques Tati)* from France
1959   **BLACK ORPHEUS** *(Marcel Camus)* from France
1960   **THE VIRGIN SPRING** *(Ingmar Bergman)* from Sweden
1961   **THROUGH A GLASS DARKLY** *(Ingmar Bergman)* from Sweden
1962   **SUNDAYS AND CYBELE** *(Serge Bourguignon)* from France
1963   **8½** *(Federico Fellini)* from Italy
1964   **YESTERDAY, TODAY AND TOMORROW** *(Vittoria De Sica)* from Italy
1965   **THE SHOP ON MAIN STREET** *(Jan Kadar/Elmar Klos)* from Czechoslovakia
1966   **UN HOMME ET UNE FEMME** *(Claude Lelouch)* from France
1967   **CLOSELY OBSERVED TRAINS** *(Jiri Menzel)* from Czechoslovakia
1968   **WAR AND PEACE** *(Sergei Bondarchuk)* from the USSR
1969   **Z** *(Constantin Costa-Gavras)* French/Algerian co-production
1970   **INVESTIGATION OF A CITIZEN ABOVE SUSPICION** *(Elio Petri)* from Italy
1971   **THE GARDEN OF THE FINZI-CONTINIS** *(Vittorio De Sica)* from Italy
1972   **THE DISCREET CHARM OF THE BOURGEOISIE** *(Luis Buñuel)* from France

Robert Basehart, Guilietta Masina

1973 **DAY FOR NIGHT** *(François Truffaut)* from France
1974 **AMARCORD** *(Federico Fellini)* from Italy
1975 **DERSU UZALA** *(Akira Kurosawa)* Japanese/USSR co-production
1976 **BLACK AND WHITE IN COLOUR** *(Jean-Jacques Annaud)*
 French/Ivory Coast co-production
1977 **MADAME ROSA** *(Moshe Mizrahi)* from France
1978 **GET OUT YOUR HANDKERCHIEFS** *(Bertrand Blier)* from France
1979 **THE TIN DRUM** *(Volker Schlöndorff)* West German/French co-
 production
1980 **MOSCOW DOES NOT BELIEVE IN TEARS** *(Vladimir Menshov)*
 from the USSR
1981 **MEPHISTO** *(István Szabó) from Hungary*

In terms of origin, these films show a clear bias to the countries of Western
Europe, although the Academy has certainly always been wide-ranging in its
search for foreign films of quality. Thus, Czechoslovakia, the USSR, a couple
of African countries via co-productions, and particularly Japan, are all
represented. Amongst foreign language directors, the Italian Vittoria De Sica
has been the most-honoured in this category, with his countryman Federico
Fellini a close second, together with the man who brought Japanese cinema to
world attention, Akira Kurosawa.

ACADEMY AWARD WINNERS

The award for the Best Original Song in a Motion Picture was first presented in 1934, and is given to the writer/composer of the song. The roles of the songs within their respective films vary considerably; many in the list below are actual main themes, heard with the credits, while others are selected from several songs within a musical production. Some are viewed on the screen, and are performed by one or more of the players, while others are heard only on the soundtrack, in a similar role to (though usually more dominant than) the customary soundtrack music. The listing shows each song's title , the writer/composer (bracketed) and the film in which it featured.

1934 **THE CONTINENTAL** *(Herb Magidson/Con Conrad)* in 'The Gay Divorce' (UK title) 'The Gay Divorcee' (in USA)

1935 **LULLABY OF BROADWAY** *(Al Dubin/Harry Warren)* in 'Gold Diggers of 1935'

1936 **THE WAY YOU LOOK TONIGHT** *(Dorothy Fields/Jerome Kern)* in 'Swing Time'

1937 **SWEET LEILANI** *(Harry Owens)* in 'Waikiki Wedding'

1938 **THANKS FOR THE MEMORY** *(Leo Robin/Ralph Rainger)* in 'The Big Broadcast of 1938'

1939 **OVER THE RAINBOW** *(E.Y. Harburg/Harold Arlen)* in 'The Wizard of Oz'

1940 **WHEN YOU WISH UPON A STAR** *(Ned Washington/Leigh Harline)* in 'Pinocchio'

1941 **THE LAST TIME I SAW PARIS** *(Oscar Hammerstein II/Jerome Kern)* in 'Lady Be Good'

1942 **WHITE CHRISTMAS** *(Irving Berlin)* in 'Holiday Inn'

1943 **YOU'LL NEVER KNOW** *(Mack Gordon/Harry Warren)* in 'Hello Frisco, Hello'

1944 **SWINGING ON A STAR** *(Johnny Burke/Jimmy Van Heusen)* in 'Going My Way'

1945 **IT MIGHT AS WELL BE SPRING** *(Richard Rodgers/Oscar Hammerstein II)* in 'State Fair'

1946 **ON THE ATCHESON, TOPEKA AND THE SANTA FE** *(Johnny Mercer/Harry Warren)* in 'The Harvey Girls'

1947 **ZIP-A-DEE-DOO-DAH** *(Ray Gilbert/Allie Wrubel)* in 'Song of the South'

1948 **BUTTONS AND BOWS** *(Jay Livingston/Ray Evans)* in 'The Paleface'

1949 **BABY, IT'S COLD OUTSIDE** *(Frank Loesser)* in 'Neptune's Daughter'

1950 **MONA LISA** *(Jay Livingston/Ray Evans)* in 'Captain Carey, USA'

1951	**IN THE COOL, COOL, COOL OF THE EVENING** *(Johnny Mercer/Hoagy Carmichael)* in 'Here Comes the Groom'
1952	**HIGH NOON** *(Ned Washington/Dmitri Tiomkin)* in 'High Noon'
1953	**SECRET LOVE** *(Paul F Webster/Sammy Fain)* in 'Calamity Jane'
1954	**THREE COINS IN THE FOUNTAIN** *(Sammy Cahn/Jule Styne)* in 'Three Coins in the Fountain'
1955	**LOVE IS A MANY SPLENDOURED THING** *(Paul F Webster/Sammy Fain)* in 'Love Is a Many Splendoured Thing'
1956	**WHATEVER WILL BE, WILL BE (QUE SERA, SERA)** *(Jay Livingston/Ray Evans)* in 'The Man Who Knew Too Much'
1957	**ALL THE WAY** *(Sammy Cahn/Jimmy Van Heusen)* in 'The Joker Is Wild'
1958	**GIGI** *(Alan Jay Lerner/Frederick Loewe)* in 'Gigi'
1959	**HIGH HOPES** *(Sammy Cahn/Jimmy Van Heusen)* in 'A Hole in the Head'
1960	**NEVER ON SUNDAY** *(Billy Towne/Manos Hadjidakis)* in 'Never on Sunday'
1961	**MOON RIVER** *(Johnny Mercer/Henry Mancini)* in 'Breakfast at Tiffany's'
1962	**DAYS OF WINE AND ROSES** *(Johnny Mercer/Henry Mancini)* in 'Days of Wine and Roses'
1963	**CALL ME IRRESPONSIBLE** *(Sammy Cahn/Jimmy Van Heusen)* in 'Papa's Delicate Condition'
1964	**CHIM CHIM CHEREE** *(Richard M Sherman/Robert B Sherman)* in 'Mary Poppins'
1965	**THE SHADOW OF YOUR SMILE** *(Paul F Webster/Johnny Mandel)* in 'The Sandpiper'
1966	**BORN FREE** *(Don Black/John Barry)* in 'Born Free'
1967	**TALK TO THE ANIMALS** *(Leslie Bricusse)* in 'Dr Dolittle'
1968	**THE WINDMILLS OF YOUR MIND** *(Alan & Marilyn Bergman/Michel Legrand)* in 'The Thomas Crown Affair'
1969	**RAINDROPS KEEP FALLIN' ON MY HEAD** *(Burt Bacharach/Hal David)* in 'Butch Cassidy and the Sundance Kid'
1970	**FOR ALL WE KNOW** *(Robb Wilson/Arthur James/Fred Karlin)* in 'Lovers and Other Strangers'

Louis Jourdan, Leslie Caron, Maurice Chevalier

Dick van Dyke, Julie Andrews

1971 **THEME FROM 'SHAFT'** *(Isaac Hayes)* in 'Shaft'
1972 **THE MORNING AFTER** *(Al Kasha/Joel Hirschhorn)* in 'The Poseidon Adventure'
1973 **THE WAY WE WERE** *(Marvin Hamlisch/Alan and Marilyn Bergman)* in 'The Way We Were'
1974 **WE MAY NEVER LOVE LIKE THIS AGAIN** *(Al Kasha/Joel Hirschhorn)* in 'The Towering Inferno'
1975 **I'M EASY** *(Keith Carradine)* in 'Nashville'
1976 **EVERGREEN** *(Barbra Streisand/Paul Williams)* in 'A Star Is Born'
1977 **YOU LIGHT UP MY LIFE** *(Joe Brooks)* in 'You Light Up My Life'
1978 **LAST DANCE** *(Paul Jabara)* in 'Thank God It's Friday'
1979 **IT GOES LIKE IT GOES** *(David Shire)* in 'Norma Rae'
1980 **FAME** *(Michael Gore/Dean Pitchford)* in 'Fame'
1981 **ARTHUR'S THEME (THE BEST THAT YOU CAN DO)** *(Christopher Cross/Carole Bayer Sager/Peter Allen/Burt Bacharach)* in 'Arthur'

With a few honourable exceptions, and disregarding the more recent films which still remain fairly solidly in the public consciousness, the most notable thing about this list of Academy Award winning song titles is that, in general, they have stood the test of time much better than the films from which they were originally taken. The man in the street might be able to hum you a snatch of 'Thanks For The Memory' or 'You'll Never Know', but how many would be able to tell you the films from which they originated — or, for that matter, have even heard of 'The Big Broadcast of 1938' or 'Hello Frisco, Hello'?

Gene Kelly and Leslie Caron

52

ACADEMY AWARD WINNERS

Best Original Film Score

The Academy's music categories were established in 1934, by which time 'talkies' had become the established norm, and every film had a soundtrack. The award for original music was later augmented by one for 'musical adaptation', where existing music (or songs) were incorporated into a score. The award is presented to the composer.

1934   **LOUIS SILVERS** for *'One Night Of Love'*
1935   **MAX STEINER** for *'The Informer'*
1936   **LEO FORBSTEIN** for *'Anthony Adverse'*
1937   **CHARLES PREVIN** for *'100 Men and a Girl'*
1938   **ERICH WOLFGANG KORNGOLD** for *'The Adventures of Robin Hood'*
1939   **HERBERT STOTHART** for *'The Wizard of Oz'*
1940   **LEIGH HARLINE/PAUL J SMITH/NED WASHINGTON** for *'Pinocchio'*

(For the next few years, the award was divided into two and awarded for both a dramatic and a musical picture. The separate categories are indicated in this list.)

1941   (Dramatic) **BERNARD HERRMANN** for *'All That Money Can Buy'*
      (Musical) **FRANK CHURCHILL/OLIVER WALLACE** for *'Dumbo'*
1942   (Dramatic) **MAX STEINER** for *'Now, Voyager'*
      (Musical) **RAY HEINDORF/HEINZ ROEMHELD** for *'Yankee Doodle Dandy'*
1943   (Dramatic) **ALFRED NEWMAN** for *'The Song of Bernadette'*
      (Musical) **RAY HEINDORF** for *'This is the Army'*
1944   (Dramatic) **MAX STEINER** for *'Since You Went Away'*
      (Musical) **CARMEN DRAGON/MORRIS STOLOFF** for *'Cover Girl'*
1945   (Dramatic) **MIKLOS ROZSA** for *'Spellbound'*
      (Musical) **GEORGIE STOLL** for *'Anchors Aweigh'*
1946   (Dramatic) **HUGO FRIEDHOFER** for *'The Best Years of Our Lives'*
      (Musical) **MORRIS STOLOFF** for *'The Jolson Story'*
1947   (Dramatic) **MIKLOS ROZSA** for *'A Double Life'*
      (Musical) **ALFRED NEWMAN** for *'Mother Wore Tights'*
1948   (Dramatic) **BRIAN EASDALE** for *'The Red Shoes'*
      (Musical) **JOHNNY GREEN/ROGER EDENS** for *'Easter Parade'*
1949   (Dramatic) **AARON COPLAND** for *'The Heiress'*
      (Musical) **ROGER EDENS/LENNIE HAYTON** for *'On The Town'*

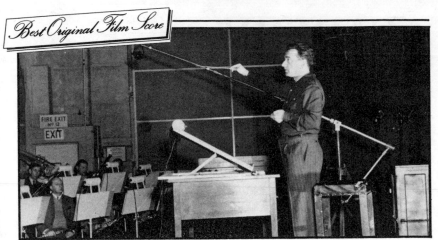

Mikos Rosza

1950	(Dramatic) **FRANZ WAXMAN** for *'Sunset Boulevard'* (Musical) **ADOLPH DEUTSCH/ROGER EDENS** for *'Annie Get Your Gun'*
1951	(Dramatic) **FRANZ WAXMAN** for *'A Place In The Sun'* (Musical) **JOHNNY GREEN/SAUL CHAPLIN** for *'An American in Paris'*
1952	(Dramatic) **DMITRI TIOMKIN** for *'High Noon'* (Musical) **ALFRED NEWMAN** for *'With a Song in My Heart'*
1953	(Dramatic) **BRONISLAU KAPER** for *'Lili'* (Musical) **ALFRED NEWMAN** for *'Call Me Madam'*
1954	(Dramatic) **DMITRI TIOMKIN** for *'The High and the Mighty'* (Musical) **ADOLPH DEUTSCH/SAUL CHAPLIN** for *'Seven Brides for Seven Brothers'*
1955	(Dramatic) **ALFRED NEWMAN** for *'Love Is a Many Splendoured Thing'* (Musical) **ROBERT RUSSELL BENNETT/JAY BLACKTON/ADOLPH DEUTSCH** for *'Oklahoma!'*
1956	(Dramatic) **VICTOR YOUNG** for *'Around The World in 80 Days'* (Musical) **ALFRED NEWMAN/KEN DARBY** for *'The King and I'*
1957	(Dramatic) **MALCOLM ARNOLD** for *'The Bridge on the River Kwai'* (There was no award for a score from a musical this year.)
1958	(Dramatic) **DMITRI TIOMKIN** for *'The Old Man and the Sea'* (Musical) **ANDRE PREVIN** for *'Gigi'*
1959	(Dramatic) **MIKLOS ROZSA** for *'Ben Hur'* (Musical) **ANDRE PREVIN/KEN DARBY** for *'Porgy and Bess'*
1960	(Dramatic) **ERNEST GOLD** for *'Exodus'* (Musical) **MORRIS STOLOFF/HARRY SUKMAN** for *'Song Without End'*
1961	(Dramatic) **HENRY MANCINI** for *'Breakfast at Tiffany's'* (Musical) **SAUL CHAPLIN/JOHNNY GREEN/SID RAMIN/IRWIN KOSTAL** for *'West Side Story'*

(From this point on, the separate categories for dramatic picture score and musical score were replaced by an award for original theme music — this was accompanied, as noted earlier, by an additional award for the best score involving existing music, which is not listed here.)

1962   **MAURICE JARRE** for *'Lawrence of Arabia'*

1963   **JOHN ADDISON** for *'Tom Jones'*

1964   **RICHARD M SHERMAN/ROBERT B SHERMAN** for *'Mary Poppins'*

1965   **MAURICE JARRE** for *'Dr Zhivago'*

1966   **JOHN BARRY** for *'Born Free'*

1967   **ELMER BERNSTEIN** for *'Thoroughly Modern Millie'*

1968   **JOHN BARRY** for *'The Lion in Winter'*

1969   **BURT BACHARACH** for *'Butch Cassidy and the Sundance Kid'*

1970   **FRANCIS LAI** for *'Love Story'*

       THE BEATLES for *'Let It Be'* (a one-off 'Best Original Song Score' award)

1971   **MICHEL LEGRAND** for *'Summer Of '42'*

1972   **CHARLES CHAPLIN/RAYMOND RASCH/LARRY RUSSELL** for *'Limelight'*

1973   **MARVIN HAMLISCH** for *'The Way We Were'*

1974   **NINO ROTA/CARMINE COPPOLA** for *'The Godfather, Part 2'*

1975   **JOHN WILLIAMS** for *'Jaws'*

1976   **JERRY GOLDSMITH** for *'The Omen'*

1977   **JOHN WILLIAMS** for *'Star Wars'*

1978   **GIORGIO MORODER** for *'Midnight Express'*

1979   **GEORGES DELERUE** for *'A Little Romance'*

1980   **MICHAEL GORE** for *'Fame'*

1981   **VANGELIS** for *'Chariots Of Fire'*

The most notable feature of this list must be the continued reappearance of certain names on the list, in complete contrast to the state of affairs which has always prevailed on the listings of best performances. This is explained in part by the fact that there were dual awards given for a considerable period of time, but it is probably also the case that producers were inclined to hire someone with a proven track record to write the score for their film if they could get him (it has never been 'her' to date), meaning that maestros of the film baton like Alfred Newman, Miklos Rozsa, Dmitri Tiomkin and Bernard Herrmann were never out of work — and rarely short of awards. John Williams, who seems to get offered every plum musical job in Hollywood these days, is obviously hell-bent on following in their footsteps.

BRITISH ACADEMY AWARDS

The British Film Academy was founded in 1946, with similar ideals to those of its already long-established American counterpart. In 1959 it merged with the Guild of Television Producers and Directors, to become known as the Society of Film and Television Arts, and then in 1975 underwent its final transformation to become the British Academy of Film and Television Arts (or BAFTA).

Though awards were given from the outset, in the early years they were low-key and few in number, with a small number of categories, and awards only being given for films themselves. The performance awards began in 1952, but it was not until 1968, when the whole system was thoroughly reorganised and incorporated into a new and prestigious ceremony along with the Television awards, that many of the categories with which we are now familiar appeared.

The Academy's award became known as the 'Stella' during the 1960s, presumably to satisfy a desire to have an appellation to match that of 'Oscar'. It hardly caught on in the same fashion, however, and reference to the term has died away noticeably in succeeding years.

Orson Welles

BRITISH ACADEMY AWARDS

From 1947 until the awards were reorganised in 1968, the British Academy presented an award to the year's best British film; in addition they presented an award for the best overall film irrespective of origin. These coincided on some occasions, but where separate films were honoured in the two categories, they are listed accordingly.
(Listings show film title, director (bracketed) and main stars.)

1947   (Overall) **THE BEST YEARS OF OUR LIVES** *(William Wyler)*
FREDRIC MARCH, MYRNA LOY
(British) **ODD MAN OUT** *(Carol Reed)*
JAMES MASON, ROBERT NEWTON
The overall winner was the 1946 best picture winner in the USA, while the UK film was a killer-on-the-run drama from the novel by F.L. Green.

1948   (Overall) **HAMLET** *(Laurence Olivier)*
LAURENCE OLIVIER, JEAN SIMMONS
(British) **THE FALLEN IDOL** *(Carol Reed)*
RALPH RICHARDSON, MICHELE MORGAN
'Hamlet' was also the American best picture winner. Reed's second domestic success was an adaptation of a Graham Greene story.

1949   (Overall) **THE BICYCLE THIEVES** *(Vittoria De Sica)*
LAMBERTO MAGGIORANI, ENZO STAIOLA
(British) **THE THIRD MAN** *(Carol Reed)*
ORSON WELLES, JOSEPH COTTEN
De Sica's warm character study against the stark background of post-war Rome is still regarded as one of the greatest films of all time. Reed's third UK winner in a row has also held up well through the decades; another Graham Greene story and a classic thriller.

1950   (Overall) **ALL ABOUT EVE** *(Joseph L Mankiewicz)*
ANNE BAXTER, BETTE DAVIS, GEORGE SANDERS
(British) **THE BLUE LAMP** *(Basil Dearden)*
JACK WARNER
Eve's portrait of a savage go-getter repeated its Oscar success, while the UK winner was the famous 'ordinary London copper' showcase which spawned TV's 'Dixon Of Dock Green'.

1951   (Overall) **LA RONDE** *(Max Ophuls)*
ANTON WALBROOK, DANIELLE DARRIEUX
(British) **THE LAVENDER HILL MOB** *(Charles Crichton)*
ALEC GUINNESS, STANLEY HOLLOWAY
The international winner was the celebrated French comedy of love's multi-sided triangle, with a host of strong players in individual segments. 'Mob' was a classic Ealing comedy taking a lighter-hearted look at the coppers 'n' crooks world than did 'The Blue Lamp'.

1952 (Both categories) **THE SOUND BARRIER** *(David Lean)*
RALPH RICHARDSON
A drama based around a now inconsequential, but then momentous,
achievement — the penetration of the sound barrier in jet flight.

1953 (Overall) **JEUX INTERDITS** *(Rene Clement)*
BRIGITTE FOSSEY, GEORGES POUJOULY
(British) **GENEVIEVE** *(Henry Cornelius)*
KENNETH MORE, KAY KENDALL
Given the English title 'Forbidden Games', Clement's film was a study of war-
torn world insanity set against the innocence of children. By contrast,
'Genevieve' was another classic British 50s comedy, the title being the name of
the central 'character' — a vintage car.

1954 (Overall) **THE WAGES OF FEAR** *(Henri-Georges Cluzot)*
YVES MONTAND, CHARLES VANEL, PETER VAN EYCK
(British) **HOBSON'S CHOICE** *(David Lean)*
CHARLES LAUGHTON, JOHN MILLS
The winner again came from France, but this time the film was a taut and
commercial thriller. The UK award went to Lean's adaption of an elderly stage
comedy of Northern industrial working-class life.

1955 (Both categories) **RICHARD III** *(Laurence Olivier)*
LAURENCE OLIVIER, JOHN GIELGUD, RALPH RICHARDSON
Olivier's third screen Shakespeare adaptation, with Olivier creating a memorable
screen image as the hunchback villainous king of the title. Oddly, the film failed
to achieve most of the nominations in the American Academy awards.

Kenneth More, Dinal Sheridan, John Gregson, Kay Kendall

Ralph Richardson, Laurence Olivier, Alec Clunes, Norman Woodland

1956   (Overall) **GERVAISE** *(Rene Clement)*
MARIA SCHELL, FRANCOIS PERIER
(British) **REACH FOR THE SKY** *(Lewis Gilbert)*
KENNETH MORE
'Gervaise' was another French production, a 19th Century drama based on an
Emile Zola novel. 'Reach For The Sky' was in the 50s British war film tradition
and related the true story of the legless air ace Douglas Bader.

1957   (Both categories) **THE BRIDGE ON THE RIVER KWAI** *(David Lean)*
ALEC GUINNESS, JACK HAWKINS, WILLIAM HOLDEN
This was the most successful British film of the decade, and one of the highest-
praised, winning many awards from both the American and the British
Academies.

1958   (Both categories) **ROOM AT THE TOP** *(Jack Clayton)*
LAURENCE HARVEY, SIMONE SIGNORET
The first fountainhead of the 'new realism' in British films, and another widely
praised production which also won several Oscar nominations and an award for
Simone Signoret.

1959   (Overall) **BEN HUR** *(William Wyler)*
CHARLTON HESTON, HUGH GRIFFITH, STEPHEN BOYD
(British) **SAPPHIRE** *(Basil Dearden)*
NIGEL PATRICK, YVONNE MITCHELL
'Ben Hur' repeated its American triumph; 'Sapphire', by contrast, was a taut and
interesting police thriller.

1960   (Overall) **THE APARTMENT** *(Billy Wilder)*
JACK LEMMON, SHIRLEY MACLAINE
(British) **SATURDAY NIGHT AND SUNDAY MORNING** *(Karel Reisz)*
ALBERT FINNEY, SHIRLEY ANN FIELD
'The Apartment' was another film to mirror its American Academy success in
Britain; the domestic winner was a fine example of the newly realistic genre of
films about working-class life.

William Holden, Jack Hawkins

1961   (Overall) **BALLAD OF A SOLDIER** *(Grigori Chukrai)*
VLADIMIR IVASHOV and
THE HUSTLER *(Robert Rossen)*
PAUL NEWMAN, JACKIE GLEASON
(British) **A TASTE OF HONEY** *(Tony Richardson)*
RITA TUSHINGHAM, DORA BRYAN, MURRAY MELVIN
The overall best film was a unique tie between a straightforward, affectionate
story from Russia, and a Paul Newman showcase in which he also won his UK
best actor award. The British winner was another well-remembered sentimental
but realistic working-class drama.

1962   (Both categories) **LAWRENCE OF ARABIA** *(David Lean)*
PETER O'TOOLE, OMAR SHARIF, ALEC GUINNESS
This lavish biography of the First World War career of T.E. Lawrence swept up
several awards, as it also did in the USA.

1963   (Both categories) **TOM JONES** *(Tony Richardson)*
ALBERT FINNEY, EDITH EVANS, HUGH GRIFFITH
Another all-British production which cleaned up the awards both in Britain and
the USA.

Best Picture

1964 (Both categories) **DR STRANGELOVE** *(Stanley Kubrick)*
PETER SELLERS, STERLING HAYDEN
For the third year running, the same film took both award categories, and in this
case the United Nations award too. The film was a biting black comedy about the
spectre of nuclear war, peopled by several Peter Sellers roles.

1965 (Overall) **MY FAIR LADY** *(George Cukor)*
REX HARRISON, AUDREY HEPBURN, STANLEY HOLLOWAY
(British) **THE IPCRESS FILE** *(Sidney Furie)*
MICHAEL CAINE, NIGEL GREEN
Cukor's musical repeated its Oscar winning success of the previous year; the
British winner was an arty but realistic espionage thriller.

1966 (Overall) **WHO'S AFRAID OF VIRGINIA WOOLF?** *(Mike Nichols)*
RICHARD BURTON, ELIZABETH TAYLOR, GEORGE SEGAL
(British) **THE SPY WHO CAME IN FROM THE COLD** *(Martin Ritt)*
RICHARD BURTON, OSKAR WERNER
Uniquely, both these films starred Richard Burton, who won the accompanying
best actor award for this performance in both roles (as did Elizabeth Taylor, his
wife at the time, for 'Woolf'). 'Spy' was a particularly bleak picture of
international espionage.

1967 (Both categories) **A MAN FOR ALL SEASONS** *(Fred Zinnemann)*
PAUL SCOFIELD, ROBERT SHAW
During the last year which gave awards for both British and Foreign productions,
both these awards ironically went to this excellent British historical film,
repeating its Oscar triumphs of the previous year.

1968 (The BAFTA reorganisation in this year narrowed the competition by
effectively halving the chances of winning an award, at least as far as
British films were concerned. Perhaps significantly, domestic
productions have figured infrequently since then.)
THE GRADUATE *(Mike Nichols)*
DUSTIN HOFFMAN, ANNE BANCROFT, KATHARINE ROSS
In the year when a British film ('Oliver!') swept the Oscars, a US production was
voted the best in Britain — Nichols' second film to win the honour.

Sterling Hayden, Peter Sellers, Stanley Kubrick

Jon Voight, Dustin Hoffman

1969 **MIDNIGHT COWBOY** *(John Schlesinger)*
JON VOIGHT, DUSTIN HOFFMAN
A magnificent British and American win for director John Schlesinger with this tragi-comic story of a would-be male stud who finds disillusionment in New York.

1970 **BUTCH CASSIDY AND THE SUNDANCE KID** *(George Roy Hill)*
PAUL NEWMAN, ROBERT REDFORD, KATHARINE ROSS
This film won nine British Academy awards, even though it had failed to carry through many of its nominations in the Oscar awards a year earlier.

1971 **SUNDAY, BLOODY SUNDAY** *(John Schlesinger)*
PETER FINCH, GLENDA JACKSON, MURRAY HEAD
This film — a keenly observed, middle-class 70s version of the love triangle — took most of the year's major British awards.

1972 **CABARET** *(Bob Fosse)*
LIZA MINNELLI, JOEL GREY
This famous musical, set in decadent pre-war Berlin, won performance awards for its stars in the USA.

1973 **DAY FOR NIGHT (LA NUIT AMERICAINE)** *(Francois Truffaut)*
JEAN-PIERRE AUMONT. JACQUELINE BISSETT
A fine French comedy about the trials and tribulations of film making and the personality clashes involved.

1974 **LACOMBE, LUCIEN** *(Louis Malle)*
PIERRE BLAISE, AURORE CLEMENT
The second French winner in a row, and also the winner of this year's United Nations award.

1975 **ALICE DOESN'T LIVE HERE ANY MORE** *(Martin Scorsese)*
ELLEN BURSTYN, KRIS KRISTOFFERSON
The film which won Ellen Burstyn her best actress award in the USA, and gave her a repeat success in Britain, in addition to taking the best film and screenplay awards.

1976 **ONE FLEW OVER THE CUCKOO'S NEST** *(Milos Forman)*
JACK NICHOLSON, LOUISE FLETCHER
This drama swept all the major awards, as it had in the USA in 1975.

1977 **ANNIE HALL** *(Woody Allen)*
WOODY ALLEN, DIANE KEATON
A duplication of this film's triumphs in the Oscar awards, it also collected best director and actress awards as well as the main prize.

1978 **JULIA** *(Fred Zinnemann)*
JANE FONDA, VANESSA REDGRAVE, JASON ROBARDS
A strong drama adapted from Lillian Hellman's story, 'Pentimento', which drew performance awards for its stars from both sides of the Atlantic.

1979 **MANHATTAN** *(Woody Allen)*
WOODY ALLEN, DIANE KEATON
Woody Allen's second win in this category, with a film more highly respected in Britain than in the USA, where it gained few nominations.

1980 **THE ELEPHANT MAN** *(David Lynch)*
ANTHONY HOPKINS, JOHN HURT
The first British film to take this award for several years was also the first black and white production to do so for a considerable time.

1981 **CHARIOTS OF FIRE** *(Hugh Hudson)*
BEN CROSS, IAN CHARLESON
The second British winner in a row, this film also took the year's Oscar and generated a new optimism in the UK film industry.

François Truffaut

BRITISH ACADEMY AWARDS

Surprisingly, the reorganisation of the BAFTA awards in 1968
introduced for the first time a category for the Best Director, and
this has remained a very important award category ever since.
As with the Best Film, there is inevitably some overlap with
recipients of the American Academy Awards, but the
individuality of British taste has left its own mark.

1968   **MIKE NICHOLS** *('The Graduate')*
The previous year's winner in the USA; Nichols strangely has made surprisingly
few films since this enduring success.

1969   **JOHN SCHLESINGER** *('Midnight Cowboy')*
A simultaneous triumph for British director Schlesinger with this Oscar success.

1970   **GEORGE ROY HILL** *('Butch Cassidy and the Sundance Kid')*
This film swept the board at the 1970 BAFTA ceremony, ironically giving Hill a
UK award three years before he won an Oscar in his native country.

1971   **JOHN SCHLESINGER** *('Sunday, Bloody Sunday')*
This film swept up most of the 1971 awards, and gave Schlesinger his second
BAFTA win.

1972   **BOB FOSSE** *('Cabaret')*
Again, this was a duplication of the American award to Fosse.

1973   **FRANCOIS TRUFFAUT** *('Day for Night')*
With 'Day for Night' also voted the best film, it was little surprise that Truffaut
should become the first European recipient of this award.

1974   **ROMAN POLANSKI** *('Chinatown')*
Polanski was nominated for, but failed to win, the American Oscar for this film
— no doubt he derived some consolation from British recognition of his work.

1975   **STANLEY KUBRICK** *('Barry Lyndon')*
Kubrick's only BAFTA award, but surprisingly one more than he has so far
received from the American Academy.

1976   **MILOS FORMAN** *('One Flew Over the Cuckoo's Nest')*
Once again, the American and British Academy judges were in full agreement
here, in their assessment of this Czech director's masterpiece.

1977   **WOODY ALLEN** *('Annie Hall')*
Another US/UK double, making it by far Allen's most popular work to date.

1978   **ALAN PARKER** *('Midnight Express')*
Parker finally brought this award back into British hands, after the hint of his
promise in the earlier 'Bugsy Malone'.

1979   **FRANCIS FORD COPPOLA** *('Apocalypse Now')*
This was another case of an American director who failed to follow through his
Oscar nomination at home, only to gain his triumph in Britain.

1980   **AKIRA KUROSAWA** *('Kagemusha')*
An epic which proved unusually successful at the box office.

1981   **LOUIS MALLE** *('Atlantic City')*
Malle's 'Lacombe, Lucien' had been voted the best film in 1974; he made the
double with the director's award for this mature Burt Lancaster showcase.

Roman Polanski

Stanley Kubrick

George Roy Hill, Robert Redford

PETER FINCH.

Peter Finch

BRITISH ACADEMY AWARDS

The British Film Academy first included categories for performer awards in 1952. These were divided into separate awards for British and Foreign performers, both actors and actresses, and were organised in this fashion for some years. Then, in 1968, a major revision was made which abolished these distinctions and reorganised the awards into straightforward Best Actor and Best Actress categories, which is how they have remained to date. The list below and the listing for Best Actress which follows it, take account of these changes and show the dual awards as made in the early years.

1952 (British) **RALPH RICHARDSON** in *'The Sound Barrier'*
(Foreign) **MARLON BRANDO** in *'Viva Zapata!'*
Richardson was of course one of Britain's most distinguished stage actors, while Brando significantly scored his first UK best actor award before he won one at home.

1953 (British) **JOHN GIELGUD** in *'Julius Caesar'*
(Foreign) **MARLON BRANDO** in *'Julius Caesar'*
The only occasion on which these awards were given to British and Foreign actors in the same film: another of the UK's great classical actors, and Brando again.

1954 (British) **KENNETH MORE** in *'Doctor in the House'*
(Foreign) **MARLON BRANDO** in *'On the Waterfront'*
The only one of these awards for More, one of the actors who personified British films of the 50s. Brando scored his third win here in a row — a record still unequalled.

1955 (British) **LAURENCE OLIVIER** in *'Richard III'*
(Foreign) **ERNEST BORGNINE** in *'Marty'*
Olivier completed the triumvirate of revered British classical stage actors to take this award, while Borgnine repeated his American triumph.

1956 (British) **PETER FINCH** in *'A Town Like Alice'*
(Foreign) **FRANÇOIS PERIER** in *'Gervaise'*
The first of many British awards for Finch, who was only honoured in the USA posthumously; and the only one for Perier — the French star of a popular Rene Clement film.

1957 (British) **ALEC GUINNESS** in *'The Bridge on the River Kwai'*
(Foreign) **HENRY FONDA** in *'Twelve Angry Men'*
It was no surprise for Guinness to repeat his Oscar triumph for his 'Kwai' role in Britain; this was Fonda's only British award, which came 24 years before his first American Oscar.

1958 (British) **TREVOR HOWARD** in *'The Key'*
(Foreign) **SIDNEY POITIER** in *'The Defiant Ones'*
Howard's win was his only award in a long and distinguished stage and screen career which continued into the 80s, while Poitier became another American to win British honours before winning an award at home.

Salvador Dali painting Olivier as Richard III

1959   (British) **PETER SELLERS** in *'I'm All Right, Jack'*
        (Foreign) **JACK LEMMON** in *'Some Like It Hot'*
        Sellers became the first comedy actor to take the British award, which made it
        appropriate that Jack Lemmon's comedy role should earn him the
        accompanying foreign honour.

1960   (British) **PETER FINCH** in *'The Trials of Oscar Wilde'*
        (Foreign) **JACK LEMMON** in *'The Apartment'*
        This was the first year in which previous winners took both British and Foreign
        categories; this was the second consecutive win for Lemmon.

1961   (British) **PETER FINCH** in *'No Love for Johnnie'*
        (Foreign) **PAUL NEWMAN** in *'The Hustler'*
        This win made Finch the most-awarded British actor to date, while Newman's
        sole British award is one more than he has had from the American Academy.

1962   (British) **PETER O'TOOLE** in *'Lawrence of Arabia'*
        (Foreign) **BURT LANCASTER** in *'The Bird Man of Alcatraz'*
        Both first time winners, these actors took awards for roles which had been
        nominated for Oscars but which had failed to win them.

1963   (British) **DIRK BOGARDE** in *'The Servant'*
        (Foreign) **MARCELLO MASTROIANNI** in *'Divorce, Italian Style'*
        One of Britain's most popular leading men of the 50s and 60s, Bogarde's first
        award was for one of his darker dramatic roles, while Italy's Mastroianni took the
        first of two successive awards.

1964   (British) **RICHARD ATTENBOROUGH** in *'Guns at Batasi'* and
        'Seance on a Wet Afternoon'
        (Foreign) **MARCELLO MASTROIANNI** in *'Yesterday, Today and
        Tomorrow'*
        Attenborough was the first actor to win on the strength of two film roles;
        Mastroianni won again in a popular De Sica film.

Alec Guinness

Dirk Bogarde

1965   (British) **DIRK BOGARDE** in *'Darling'*
        (Foreign) **LEE MARVIN** in *'The Killers'* and *'Cat Ballou'*
        Bogarde's second win, for the film in which his co-star Julie Christie collected an
        American Oscar. Marvin, in contrasting roles, was the first American actor to
        score from two films.

1966   (British) **RICHARD BURTON** in *'The Spy Who Came in from the
        Cold'* and *'Who's Afraid of Virginia Woolf?'*
        (Foreign) **ROD STEIGER** in *'The Pawnbroker'*
        The only win for Burton (though for two performances), while Steiger's award
        came a year before he took the Oscar in the USA.

1967   (British) **PAUL SCOFIELD** in *'A Man for All Seasons'*
        (Foreign) **ROD STEIGER** in *'In the Heat of the Night'*
        In the last year of dual awards, Steiger duplicated his American success, as did
        Scofield from the previous year.

Best Actor

(From this point onwards, the British and Foreign categories were combined)

1968   **SPENCER TRACY** in *'Guess Who's Coming to Dinner?'*
With competition in the awards increased two-fold, Tracy took the posthumous honour, for which he was nominated but not awarded in the USA.

1969   **DUSTIN HOFFMAN** in *'Midnight Cowboy'* and *'John and Mary'*
The first of a slew of winners in multiple roles. Hoffman's success came a decade before his American Oscar.

1970   **ROBERT REDFORD** in *'Butch Cassidy and the Sundance Kid'* and *'Tell Them Willie Boy Is Here'*
Another dual win by a man who, despite being one of the top box office stars in the 70s, has never won an American best actor award.

1971   **PETER FINCH** in *'Sunday, Bloody Sunday'*
Finch's fourth win, for his much acclaimed role as the bemused middle-aged member of an odd love triangle.

1972   **GENE HACKMAN** in *'The French Connection'* and *'The Poseidon Adventure'*
Hackman's splendid portrayal of an obsessive New York narcotics agent, which had also won him an Oscar the previous year.

1973   **WALTER MATTHAU** in *'Pete 'n' Tillie'* and *'Charley Varrick'*
Matthau, a long-established actor of sophisticated comedy roles, here won awards for two diverse parts giving him his only acting awards to date.

1974   **JACK NICHOLSON** in *'Chinatown'* and *'The Last Detail'*
Another award for dual roles: Nicholson's part in the harsh 1930s thriller 'Chinatown' made a huge impact with both critics and audiences in Britain.

1975   **AL PACINO** in *'The Godfather Part II'* and *'Dog Day Afternoon'*
Pacino was awarded here for two roles — for which he had been unsuccessfully nominated for an Oscar in the USA both this year and the previous one.

1976   **JACK NICHOLSON** in *'One Flew Over the Cuckoo's Nest'*
The second win for Nicholson in the darkly comic role of a mental patient, and a repeat of his 1975 American success.

1977   **PETER FINCH** in *'Network'*
Finch's fifth award, given posthumously, for the role which also won him his Oscar.

1978   **RICHARD DREYFUSS** in *'The Goodbye Girl'*
Dreyfuss, a huge box office star by the end of the decade, here repeated his Oscar success of the previous year.

1979   **JACK LEMMON** in *'The China Syndrome'*
Lemmon's first UK award in 20 years, this time for a dramatic role.

1980   **JOHN HURT** in *'The Elephant Man'*
The only British actor, apart from Peter Finch, to win the combined best actor award to date. Hurt's triumphant role was possibly the most obscured by make-up ever.

1981   **BURT LANCASTER** in *'Atlantic City'*
Lancaster's second UK award, after a lapse of almost 20 years, for his role in the film which also gave Louis Malle the best director award.

It can be seen from this list that Peter Finch, with five awards, has been the actor most decorated by the British Academy to date. It is also notable that since the domestic and foreign categories were combined, American actors have taken most of the awards.

Simone Signoret

BRITISH ACADEMY AWARDS

(For notes pertinent to this listing, see the paragraph at the head of the Best Actor category, since the same time scale and change of awards procedure apply.)

1952   (British) **VIVIEN LEIGH** in *'A Streetcar Named Desire'*
(Foreign) **SIMONE SIGNORET** in *'Casque D'Or'*
Vivien Leigh repeated her previous year's American Oscar success, while this was the first of several wins for accomplished French actress Simone Signoret.

1953   (British) **AUDREY HEPBURN** in *'Roman Holiday'*
(Foreign) **LESLIE CARON** in *'Lili'*
Leslie Caron, an early protegée of Gene Kelly, moved into light film roles and later settled in the UK. Audrey Hepburn's award was a repeat of her Oscar success and came in only her third year in films.

1954   (British) **YVONNE MITCHELL** in *'The Divided Heart'*
(Foreign) **CORNELL BORCHERS** in *'The Divided Heart'*
As had happened the previous year in the best actor awards, both these recipients were in the same film, which also won the United Nations Award.

1955   (British) **KATIE JOHNSON** in *'The Ladykillers'*
(Foreign) **BETSY BLAIR** in *'Marty'*
Katie Johnson's only award was for her role opposite Alec Guinness in this black comedy, while Betsy Blair achieved a win for which she was not even nominated in the USA.

1956   (British) **VIRGINIA McKENNA** in *'A Town Like Alice'*
(Foreign) **ANNA MAGNANI** in *'The Rose Tattoo'*
McKenna was a popular UK leading lady from early showcases like 'The Cruel Sea' and 'Born Free' in the 60s. Italy's Anna Magnani repeated her American success in 'The Rose Tattoo'.

1957   (British) **HEATHER SEARS** in *'The Story of Esther Costello'*
(Foreign) **SIMONE SIGNORET** in *'Witches of Salem'*
Heather Sears won the award in only her second starring film role after long experience on the stage. France's Simone Signoret won her second award in a film version of the famous true story of the Salem witchcraft trials.

1958   (British) **IRENE WORTH** in *'Orders to Kill'*
(Foreign) **SIMONE SIGNORET** in *'Room at the Top'*
Irene Worth came originally from the USA but latterly worked in Britain, mainly on the stage. Simone Signoret's third award was for her best-remembered role as the mistress of Laurence Harvey's young go-getter.

1959   (British) **AUDREY HEPBURN** in *'The Nun's Story'*
(Foreign) **SHIRLEY MacLAINE** in *'Ask Any Girl'*
The second of Audrey Hepburn's wins, with a role for which she was also nominated for an Oscar, and the first of two successive awards for America's Shirley MacLaine.

1960   (British) **RACHEL ROBERTS** in *'Saturday Night and Sunday Morning'*
(Foreign) **SHIRLEY MacLAINE** in *'The Apartment'*
Rachel Roberts was another well-known stage actress who had made few films prior to this, while Shirley MacLaine's award was one of the many awards received by 'The Apartment'.

Audrey Hepburn

Julie Christie

1961   (British) **DORA BRYAN** in *'A Taste of Honey'*
       (Foreign) **SOPHIA LOREN** in *'Two Women'*
       Dora Bryan, best known as a comedy character actress, greatly deserved this
       win; Sophia Loren repeated her American Academy Award success.

1962   (British) **LESLIE CARON** in *'The L-Shaped Room'*
       (Foreign) **ANNE BANCROFT** in *'The Miracle Worker'*
       Leslie Caron won her award for her part in another of Britain's new spate of
       realistic dramas, while Anne Bancroft repeated her US success with a return to
       the cinema after a long stint on Broadway.

1963   (British) **RACHEL ROBERTS** in *'This Sporting Life'*
       (Foreign) **PATRICIA NEAL** in *'Hud'*
       Rachel Roberts had made few films prior to her strong parts in gritty dramas like
       this one and 'Saturday Night and Sunday Morning', concentrating instead on
       stage work. Patricia Neal's award was for her dramatic performance opposite
       Paul Newman.

Elizabeth Taylor

1964　(British) **AUDREY HEPBURN** in *'Charade'*
(Foreign) **ANNE BANCROFT** in *'The Pumpkin Eater'*
Audrey Hepburn, completed her trio of awards with another dramatic role,
while Anne Bancroft scored for the second time (and also won an American
nomination).

1965　(British) **JULIE CHRISTIE** in *'Darling'*
(Foreign) **PATRICIA NEAL** in *'In Harm's Way'*
Julie Christie's role as the ambitious young female in swingin' England brought
her to world attention. Patricia Neal, in another gritty drama, achieved the
second award she had failed to win in the USA.

1966　(British) **ELIZABETH TAYLOR** in *'Who's Afraid of Virginia Woolf?'*
(Foreign) **JEANNE MOREAU** in *'Viva Maria'*
Elizabeth Taylor was finally honoured in Britain after many years as a top star,
while France's respected Jeanne Moreau won playing a lighter role than usual.

1967　(British) **EDITH EVANS** in *'The Whisperers'*
(Foreign) **ANOUK AIMEE** in *'A Man and a Woman'*
Veteran British classical actress Edith Evans achieved her only best film actress
award in 'The Whisperers'; Anouk Aimee's win testified to the international
popularity of 'Un Homme et Une Femme'.

(From this point onwards, the British and Foreign categories were combined.)

1968 **KATHARINE HEPBURN** in *'Guess Who's Coming to Dinner?'* and *'The Lion in Winter'*
With the awards combined, Katharine Hepburn ironically triumphed with wins for contrasting roles, in a domestic drama and a historical piece.

1969 **MAGGIE SMITH** in *'The Prime of Miss Jean Brodie'*
Maggie Smith was the first British winner of the combined categories, with her acclaimed performance as the prim but confused schoolmistress.

1970 **KATHARINE ROSS** in *'Butch Cassidy and the Sundance Kid'* and *'Tell Them Willie Boy Is Here'*
The second dual award went to an actress who has never won best actress in her own country.

1971 **GLENDA JACKSON** in *'Sunday, Bloody Sunday'*
A year after her 'Women In Love' Oscar, Glenda won her only UK best actress award for her part as the woman who shared two men in the much acclaimed film of D.H. Lawrence's novel.

1972 **LIZA MINNELLI** in *'Cabaret'*
Liza Minnelli also won an Oscar, for another much-honoured film.

1973 **STEPHANE AUDRAN** in *'The Discreet Charm of the Bourgeoisie'* and *'Juste Avant La Nuit'*
The first European winner of this combined award, from France, and again for two roles.

1974 **JOANNE WOODWARD** in *'Summer Wishes, Winter Dreams'*
Joanne Woodward here scored her first major award since her sole Oscar in 1957.

1975 **ELLEN BURSTYN** in *'Alice Doesn't Live Here Any More'*
Ellen Burstyn repeated her previous year's Oscar win in the role of a mother who walks out of a hopeless marriage, with her child, in search of a better future.

1976 **LOUISE FLETCHER** in *'One Flew Over The Cuckoo's Nest'*
Another repeat of the previous year's Oscar win for Louise Fletcher's much-acclaimed performance opposite Jack Nicholson.

1977 **DIANE KEATON** in *'Annie Hall'*
For the film 'Annie Hall' which won many awards, this was another American/British win.

1978 **JANE FONDA** in *'Julia'*
A strong role alongside Vanessa Redgrave in the autobiographical story of Lillian Hellman gave Jane Fonda her first UK best actress award.

1979 **JANE FONDA** in *'The China Syndrome'*
The second successive Fonda win, and again for a role whose nomination did not succeed in the USA.

1980 **JUDY DAVIS** in *'My Brilliant Career'*
In one of her first roles, this Australian actress made a significant impact in a dramatic story played against the background of her native country.

1981 **MERYL STREEP** in *'The French Lieutenant's Woman'*
Meryl Streep had already won a supporting actress Oscar for 'Kramer Vs. Kramer'; this film gave her her first triumph in the lead role.

Fred Astaire

BRITISH ACADEMY AWARDS

Timothy Bottoms and
Ben Johnson

As with several of the BAFTA award categories later to assume
paramount importance (from both an artist's and a critic's point
of view), the Best Supporting Actor and Actress awards were
not introduced until 1968 when the award giving ceremony was
reorganised. Awards for male and female artists were kept
segregated until the Best Supporting Artist's award was
introduced in 1981. Since the first winner of this combined
category was Ian Holm, his listing is included at the foot of the
Best Supporting Actor section below, rather than in a new list all
by himself.

1968   **IAN HOLM** (in *'The Bofors Gun'*)
1969   **LAURENCE OLIVIER** (in *'Oh! What a Lovely War!'*)
1970   **COLIN WELLAND** (in *'Kes'*)
1971   **EDWARD FOX** (in *'The Go-Between'*)
1972   **BEN JOHNSON** (in *'The Last Picture Show'*)
1973   **ARTHUR LOWE** (in *'O Lucky Man'*)
1974   **JOHN GIELGUD** (in *'Murder on the Orient Express'*)
1975   **FRED ASTAIRE** (in *'The Towering Inferno'*)
1976   **BRAD DOURIF** (in *'One Flew Over the Cuckoo's Nest'*)
1977   **EDWARD FOX** (in *'A Bridge Too Far'*)
1978   **JOHN HURT** (in *'Midnight Express'*)
1979   **ROBERT DUVALL** (in *'Apocalypse Now'*)
        (The last 'Best Supporting Actor' award)

BEST SUPPORTING ARTIST

1981   **JO PESCI** (in *'Raging Bull'*)

Susannah York

84

BRITISH ACADEMY AWARDS

Ingrid Bergman

Like those for their male counterparts, the Best Supporting Actress Awards were first given in 1968. They were superseded in the most recent ceremony by a 'Best Supporting Artist' award. (See Best Supporting Actor — opening note.)

1968   **BILLIE WHITELAW** (in 'The Twisted Nerve' and 'Charlie Bubbles')
1969   **CELIA JOHNSON** (in 'The Prime of Miss Jean Brodie')
1970   **SUSANNAH YORK** (in 'They Shoot Horses, Don't They?')
1971   **MARGARET LEIGHTON** (in 'The Go-Between')
1972   **CLORIS LEACHMAN** (in 'The Last Picture Show')
1973   **VALENTINA CORTESE** (in 'Day For Night')
1974   **INGRID BERGMAN** (in 'Murder on the Orient Express')
1975   **DIANE LADD** (in 'Alice Doesn't Live Here Any More')
1976   **JODIE FOSTER** (in 'Bugsy Malone' and 'Taxi Driver')
1977   **JENNY AGUTTER** (in 'Equus')
1978   **GERALDINE PAGE** (in 'Interiors')
1979   **RACHEL ROBERTS** (in 'Yanks')
        (The last 'Best Supporting Actress' award)

Emmanuelle Riva

BRITISH ACADEMY AWARDS – UNITED NATIONS AWARD

A feature of the British Academy awards from 1949 until 1975, the United Nations Award was given using somewhat different cirteria from the other presentations. It was awarded to a film which in some positive way embodied one or more of the principles of the United Nations charter. Taking into consideration themes such as human rights, religious freedom, emancipation, freedom of speech, and the promotion of co-operation between nations rather than strife, readers may find it interesting to try puzzling out just which of its principles the UN found embodied in some of these films.

1949   **THE SEARCH** *(Fred Zinnemann)*
A postwar drama telling of the relationship between a US soldier and a German war orphan.

1950   **INTRUDER IN THE DUST** *(Clarence Brown)*
A murder mystery and legal intrigue which also sheds a positive light on a black/white relationship in America's South.

1951   **FOUR IN A JEEP** *(Leopold Lindtberg)*
Another early postwar political comment showing the suspicions and divisions between 'allies' in an international police team in Vienna.

1952   **CRY THE BELOVED COUNTRY** *(Zoltan Korda)*
An earnest fable of the friendship between a black and a white man in South Africa.

1953   **WORLD WITHOUT END** *(Film not known to the compilers)*

1954   **THE DIVIDED HEART** *(Charles Crichton)*
A 'tug-of-love' theme involving a war 'orphan', his foster parents, and his lately reappeared real mother.

1955   **CHILDREN OF HIROSHIMA** *(Kaneto Shindo)*
A dramatised semi-documentary of life in Hiroshima in the years after the Atomic Bomb.

1956   **RACE FOR LIFE** *(Film not known to the compilers)*

1957   **THE HAPPY ROAD** *(Gene Kelly)*
A comedy pointing at the misunderstandings which exist between the adult generation and their children.

1958   **THE DEFIANT ONES** *(Stanley Kramer)*
The story of a black and a white convict on the run, mutually hating yet needing to survive together.

1959   **ON THE BEACH** *(Stanley Kramer)*
A sombre story of civilization's last respite in Australia after an atomic war, as windblown radioactive dust sets the time limit for survival.

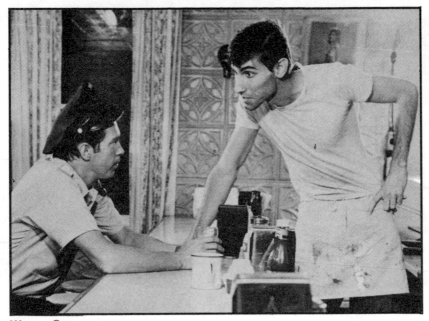

Warren Oates

1960 **HIROSHIMA, MON AMOUR** *(Alain Resnais)*
A love affair in post-war Hiroshima between a French woman and a Japanese man, conjuring up wartime memories.

1961 **LET MY PEOPLE GO** *(Film not known to the compilers)*

1962 **REACH FOR GLORY** *(Philip Leacock)*
A sombre warning fable of the corruption of childhood innocence by worldly insanity, in a Second World War setting.

1963 **INHERITANCE** *(Film not known to the compilers)*

1964 **DR STRANGELOVE** *(Stanley Kubrick)*
Kubrick's famous dark comedy about a multiplicity of men's follies bringing about the nuclear holocaust.

1965 **TOKYO OLYMPIAD** *(Kon Ichikawa)*
A stirringly filmed account of the 1964 Tokyo Olympic Games.

1966 **THE WAR GAME** *(Peter Watkins)*
Originally made for TV, this film shows, in documentary style, the aftermath of a fictitious Nuclear attack on Britain.

1967 **IN THE HEAT OF THE NIGHT** *(Norman Jewison)*
One of the best-known films to have won this award, with two characters symbolising black/white racial tension whilst solving a murder.

1968 **GUESS WHO'S COMING TO DINNER?** *(Stanley Kramer)*
Another famous study of race relationships, this time in a domestic setting.

1969 **OH! WHAT A LOVELY WAR!** *(Richard Attenborough)*
A savage satire on the folly of World War One, heightened by its treatment as a lively musical.

1970 **M*A*S*H** *(Robert Altman)*
Famous comedy centred around a field medical unit in the Korean War, with a liberal dousing of anti-war satire.

1971 **THE BATTLE OF ALGIERS** *(Gillo Pontecorvo)*
A story of the 1950s Algerian terrorist uprising against the territory's French colonial masters.

1972   **THE GARDEN OF THE FINZI-CONTINIS** *(Vittorio De Sica)*
The collapse of the pre-war world of a family of wealthy Jewish Italians, in the face of the Nazi holocaust.

1973   **STATE OF SIEGE** *(Constantin Costa-Gavras)*
A film not known in detail to the compilers, but made by the inventive, politically-aware director of 'Z'.

1974   **LACOMBE LUCIEN** *(Louis Malle)*
A character study set against the background of Nazi Germany.

1975   **CONRACK** *(Martin Ritt)*
Another racial study, featuring a white teacher in an all-black Southern USA school, and taking an optimistic view.

At this point, the United Nations Award category was discontinued. Cynically, it might be wondered whether the judges were finding it increasingly difficult to find well-made films which also embodied a requisite of the award, rather than exploiting negative aspects of the Human Condition.

As the listing shows, some of the honours were given to fairly obscure productions, and the compilers apologise for not being able to give full identification of some of these little-known items.

THE TOP 50 MOST POPULAR BOX OFFICE STARS, 1930 – 1980

A full tabulation of all the Quigley Annual Top Ten Box Office lists provides a rank order listing of the most consistently popular movie figures in the last 50 years. Again, this is to some extent trying to quantify the unquantifiable, but accepting that there is no way that comparative popularity can be measured with absolute accuracy, the listing does present a logical and acceptable — and extremely interesting — picture. John Wayne's tabulations total is so far in advance of the closest opposition, that there can be absolutely no doubt of his position as the top box office draw over the last 50 years. Many of the more recent names, still actively making successful films, poll fairly low simply because they have not yet had the opportunity to appear in sufficient annual Top Ten lists to challenge the veterans — they can be expected to change the overall pattern considerably in forthcoming years.

It should be borne in mind that only artists who achieved a Top Ten placing in any year have had their scores tabulated. Anyone who stood at a hypothetical number 11 position in the list for years on end should undoubtedly be in here as well, but there is no way of assessing this. The figure to the right of each listing shows the total number of years in which that person appeared in the annual Top Ten lists. Again, Wayne has no real challengers in these longevity stakes.

John Wayne

Cary Grant

Elizabeth Taylor and Robert Taylor

1	**JOHN WAYNE**	25		26	**WILLIAM HOLDEN**	6
2	**BING CROSBY**	15		27	**DUSTIN HOFFMAN**	6
3	**GARY COOPER**	18		28	**WILL ROGERS**	4
4	**CLINT EASTWOOD**	13		29	**ELVIS PRESLEY**	7
5	**CLARK GABLE**	16		30	**SEAN CONNERY**	4
6	**BOB HOPE**	13		31	**JANET GAYNOR**	3
7	**PAUL NEWMAN**	12		32	**JOAN CRAWFORD**	5
8	**DORIS DAY**	10		33	**GREER GARSON**	5
9	**ROCK HUDSON**	8		34	**WALLACE BEERY**	5
10	**BETTY GRABLE**	9		35	**MARIE DRESSLER**	3
11	**CARY GRANT**	11		36	**GLENN FORD**	3
12	**BURT REYNOLDS**	9		37	**JERRY LEWIS** (solo)	6
13	**ABBOTT & COSTELLO**	8		38	**LEE MARVIN**	5
14	**JAMES STEWART**	10		39	**ROBERT TAYLOR**	3
15	**ROBERT REDFORD**	6		40	**SIDNEY POITIER**	3
16	**ELIZABETH TAYLOR**	9		41	**FRED ASTAIRE &**	
17	**SHIRLEY TEMPLE**	6			**GINGER ROGERS**	3
18	**BARBRA STREISAND**	8		42	**MARLON BRANDO**	6
19	**SPENCER TRACY**	10		43	**INGRID BERGMAN**	3
20	**STEVE McQUEEN**	9		44	**JOHN TRAVOLTA**	3
21	**MICKEY ROONEY**	6		45	**JANE FONDA**	3
22	**DEAN MARTIN &**			46	**FRANK SINATRA**	6
	JERRY LEWIS	6		47	**JAMES CAGNEY**	7
23	**JACK LEMMON**	8		48	**VAN JOHNSON**	2
24	**JULIE ANDREWS**	4		49	**AL PACINO**	4
25	**HUMPHREY BOGART**	8		50	**TYRONE POWER**	3

There are two duos included here; half of one of them — Jerry Lewis — also appears 15 places lower as a result of his solo film success after parting from Dean Martin. Lewis is the only artist to have achieved a double chart entry. Several other renowned cinematic duos — Laurel and Hardy probably being the most obvious example — are nowhere to be seen.

The balance of the top 50 leans heavily towards male dominance, as do most of the individual annual listings. Of the ladies in the upper reaches, only Barbra Streisand, as an active top box office star, looks likely to improve her position a few years hence, although there is also plenty of film life left yet in the likes of Julie Andrews and Jane Fonda.

At the very top, the four men placed around Clint Eastwood are now all dead, and he only needs to continue his current output of a blockbuster a year for a while longer to haul himself into runner-up position behind John Wayne. That Wayne's quarter-century of supremacy can ever be equalled or surpassed, even by Eastwood or the fast-rising Burt Reynolds, seems unlikely.

Fred Astaire and Ginger Rogers

THE ANNUAL TOP TEN BOX OFFICE STARS, 1932 – 1980

These listings are adapted from annual polls conducted amongst film exhibitors in the USA by Quigley Publications. Those polled are asked to list the year's top box office stars according to the amount of business their films have generated through the individual outlets. The results provide an assessment rather than a totally accurate audit of box office popularity, and they do obviously favour prolific film makers rather than those stars whose appeal may be huge but whose films are infrequent.

Since the results are tabulated from within the USA, they obviously only measure American box office tastes, but as no comparable poll has been taken consistently in Britain or elsewhere, this must serve as a general historical review. In fact, it has remained true through most of the half-century covered here that cinema tastes throughout the English-speaking world have fairly closely mirrored those of the USA — particularly in terms of the popularity of the biggest star names.

The annual lists which follow show the individuals' rank order; a bracketed reminder of the previous year's position, and (to the far right) the accumulated total of years in which a star has featured on the Top Ten. This allows the rise and fall of individual popularity to be followed through the years.

Bud Abbott and Lou Costello

1932

1	MARIE DRESSLER	1
2	JANET GAYNOR	1
3	JOAN CRAWFORD	1
4	CHARLES FARRELL	1
5	GRETA GARBO	1
6	NORMA SHEARER	1
7	WALLACE BEERY	1
8	CLARK GABLE	1
9	WILL ROGERS	1
10	JOE E BROWN	1

1933

1	(1)	MARIE DRESSLER	2
2	(9)	WILL ROGERS	2
3	(2)	JANET GAYNOR	2
4	(-)	EDDIE CANTOR	1
5	(7)	WALLACE BEERY	2
6	(-)	JEAN HARLOW	1
7	(8)	CLARK GABLE	2
8	(-)	MAE WEST	1
9	(6)	NORMA SHEARER	2
10	(3)	JOAN CRAWFORD	2

1934

1	(2)	WILL ROGERS	3
2	(7)	CLARK GABLE	3
3	(3)	JANET GAYNOR	3
4	(5)	WALLACE BEERY	3
5	(8)	MAE WEST	2
6	(10)	JOAN CRAWFORD	3
7	(-)	BING CROSBY	1
8	(-)	SHIRLEY TEMPLE	1
9	(1)	MARIE DRESSLER	3
10	(9)	NORMA SHEARER	9

1935

1	(8)	SHIRLEY TEMPLE	2
2	(1)	WILL ROGERS	4
3	(2)	CLARK GABLE	4
4	(-)	ASTAIRE & ROGERS	1
5	(6)	JOAN CRAWFORD	4
6	(-)	CLAUDETTE COLBERT	1
7	(-)	DICK POWELL	1
8	(4)	WALLACE BEERY	4
9	(-)	JOE E BROWN	2
10	(-)	JAMES CAGNEY	1

1936

1	(1)	SHIRLEY TEMPLE	3
2	(3)	CLARK GABLE	5
3	(4)	ASTAIRE & ROGERS	2
4	(-)	ROBERT TAYLOR	1
5	(9)	JOE E BROWN	3
6	(7)	DICK POWELL	2
7	(5)	JOAN CRAWFORD	5
8	(6)	CLAUDETTE COLBERT	2
9	(-)	JEANETTE MacDONALD	1
10	(-)	GARY COOPER	1

1937

1	(1)	SHIRLEY TEMPLE	4
2	(2)	CLARK GABLE	6
3	(4)	ROBERT TAYLOR	2
4	(-)	BING CROSBY	2
5	(-)	WILLIAM POWELL	1
6	(-)	JANE WITHERS	1
7	(3)	ASTAIRE & ROGERS	3
8	(-)	SONJA HENIE	1
9	(10)	GARY COOPER	2
10	(-)	MYRNA LOY	1

1938

1	(1)	SHIRLEY TEMPLE	5
2	(2)	CLARK GABLE	7
3	(8)	SONJA HENIE	2
4	(-)	MICKEY ROONEY	1
5	(-)	SPENCER TRACY	1
6	(3)	ROBERT TAYLOR	3
7	(10)	MYRNA LOY	2
8	(6)	JANE WITHERS	2
9	(-)	ALICE FAYE	1
10	(-)	TYRONE POWER	1

1939

1	(4)	MICKEY ROONEY	2
2	(10)	TYRONE POWER	2
3	(5)	SPENCER TRACY	2
4	(2)	CLARK GABLE	8
5	(1)	SHIRLEY TEMPLE	6
6	(-)	BETTE DAVIS	1
7	(9)	ALICE FAYE	2
8	(-)	ERROL FLYNN	1
9	(-)	JAMES CAGNEY	2
10	(3)	SONJA HENIE	3

Bob Hope and Dorothy Lamour

1940

1	(1)	**MICKEY ROONEY**	3
2	(3)	**SPENCER TRACY**	3
3	(4)	**CLARK GABLE**	9
4	(-)	**GENE AUTRY**	1
5	(2)	**TYRONE POWER**	3
6	(9)	**JAMES CAGNEY**	3
7	(-)	**BING CROSBY**	3
8	(-)	**WALLACE BEERY**	5
9	(6)	**BETTE DAVIS**	2
10	(-)	**JUDY GARLAND**	1

1941

1	(1)	**MICKEY ROONEY**	4
2	(3)	**CLARK GABLE**	10
3	(-)	**ABBOTT & COSTELLO**	1
4	(-)	**BOB HOPE**	1
5	(2)	**SPENCER TRACY**	4
6	(4)	**GENE AUTRY**	2
7	(-)	**GARY COOPER**	3
8	(9)	**BETTE DAVIS**	3
9	(6)	**JAMES CAGNEY**	4
10	(10)	**JUDY GARLAND**	2

1942

1	(3)	**ABBOTT & COSTELLO**	2
2	(2)	**CLARK GABLE**	11
3	(7)	**GARY COOPER**	4
4	(1)	**MICKEY ROONEY**	5
5	(4)	**BOB HOPE**	2
6	(9)	**JAMES CAGNEY**	5
7	(6)	**GENE AUTRY**	3
8	(-)	**BETTY GRABLE**	1
9	(-)	**GREER GARSON**	1
10	(5)	**SPENCER TRACY**	5

1943

1	(8)	**BETTY GRABLE**	2
2	(5)	**BOB HOPE**	3
3	(1)	**ABBOTT & COSTELLO**	3
4	(-)	**BING CROSBY**	4
5	(3)	**GARY COOPER**	5
6	(9)	**GREER GARSON**	2
7	(-)	**HUMPHREY BOGART**	1
8	(6)	**JAMES CAGNEY**	6
9	(4)	**MICKEY ROONEY**	6
10	(2)	**CLARK GABLE**	12

1944

1	(4)	**BING CROSBY**	5
2	(5)	**GARY COOPER**	6
3	(2)	**BOB HOPE**	4
4	(1)	**BETTY GRABLE**	3
5	(-)	**SPENCER TRACY**	6
6	(6)	**GREER GARSON**	3
7	(7)	**HUMPHREY BOGART**	2
8	(3)	**ABBOTT & COSTELLO**	4
9	(-)	**CARY GRANT**	1
10	(-)	**BETTE DAVIS**	4

1945

1	(1)	**BING CROSBY**	6
2	(-)	**VAN JOHNSON**	1
3	(6)	**GREER GARSON**	4
4	(4)	**BETTY GRABLE**	4
5	(5)	**SPENCER TRACY**	7
6	(7)	**HUMPHREY BOGART**	3
7	(2)	**GARY COOPER**	7
8	(3)	**BOB HOPE**	5
9	(-)	**JUDY GARLAND**	3
10	(-)	**MARGARET O'BRIEN**	1

1946

1	(1)	**BING CROSBY**	7
2	(-)	**INGRID BERGMAN**	1
3	(2)	**VAN JOHNSON**	2
4	(6)	**GARY COOPER**	8
5	(8)	**BOB HOPE**	6
6	(6)	**HUMPHREY BOGART**	4
7	(3)	**GREER GARSON**	5
8	(10)	**MARGARET O'BRIEN**	2
9	(4)	**BETTY GRABLE**	5
10	(-)	**ROY ROGERS**	1

1947

1	(1)	**BING CROSBY**	8
2	(9)	**BETTY GRABLE**	6
3	(2)	**INGRID BERGMAN**	2
4	(4)	**GARY COOPER**	9
5	(6)	**HUMPHREY BOGART**	5
6	(5)	**BOB HOPE**	7
7	(-)	**CLARK GABLE**	13
8	(-)	**GREGORY PECK**	1
9	(-)	**CLAUDETTE COLBERT**	3
10	(-)	**ALAN LADD**	1

1948

1	(1)	**BING CROSBY**	9
2	(2)	**BETTY GRABLE**	7
3	(-)	**ABBOTT & COSTELLO**	5
4	(4)	**GARY COOPER**	10
5	(6)	**BOB HOPE**	8
6	(5)	**HUMPHREY BOGART**	6
7	(7)	**CLARK GABLE**	14
8	(-)	**CARY GRANT**	2
9	(-)	**SPENCER TRACY**	8
10	(3)	**INGRID BERGMAN**	3

1949

1	(5)	**BOB HOPE**	9
2	(1)	**BING CROSBY**	10
3	(3)	**ABBOTT & COSTELLO**	6
4	(-)	**JOHN WAYNE**	1
5	(4)	**GARY COOPER**	11
6	(8)	**CARY GRANT**	3
7	(2)	**BETTY GRABLE**	8
8	(-)	**ESTHER WILLIAMS**	1
9	(6)	**HUMPHREY BOGART**	7
10	(7)	**CLARK GABLE**	15

1950

1	(4)	**JOHN WAYNE**	2
2	(1)	**BOB HOPE**	10
3	(2)	**BING CROSBY**	11
4	(7)	**BETTY GRABLE**	9
5	(-)	**JAMES STEWART**	1
6	(3)	**ABBOTT & COSTELLO**	7
7	(-)	**CLIFTON WEBB**	1
8	(8)	**ESTHER WILLIAMS**	2
9	(-)	**SPENCER TRACY**	9
10	(-)	**RANDOLPH SCOTT**	1

1951

1	(1)	**JOHN WAYNE**	3
2	(-)	**MARTIN & LEWIS**	1
3	(4)	**BETTY GRABLE**	9
4	(6)	**ABBOTT & COSTELLO**	8
5	(3)	**BING CROSBY**	12
6	(2)	**BOB HOPE**	11
7	(10)	**RANDOLPH SCOTT**	2
8	(-)	**GARY COOPER**	12
9	(-)	**DORIS DAY**	1
10	(9)	**SPENCER TRACY**	10

James Stewart

Dean Martin and Friends

Marilyn Monroe

1952

1	(2)	**MARTIN & LEWIS**	2
2	(8)	**GARY COOPER**	13
3	(1)	**JOHN WAYNE**	4
4	(5)	**BING CROSBY**	13
5	(6)	**BOB HOPE**	12
6	(-)	**JAMES STEWART**	2
7	(9)	**DORIS DAY**	2
8	(-)	**GREGORY PECK**	2
9	(-)	**SUSAN HAYWARD**	1
10	(7)	**RANDOLPH SCOTT**	3

1953

1	(2)	**GARY COOPER**	14
2	(1)	**MARTIN & LEWIS**	3
3	(3)	**JOHN WAYNE**	5
4	(-)	**ALAN LADD**	2
5	(4)	**BING CROSBY**	14
6	(-)	**MARILYN MONROE**	1
7	(6)	**JAMES STEWART**	3
8	(5)	**BOB HOPE**	(13)
9	(9)	**SUSAN HAYWARD**	2
10	(10)	**RANDOLPH SCOTT**	4

1954

1	(3)	**JOHN WAYNE**	6
2	(2)	**MARTIN & LEWIS**	4
3	(1)	**GARY COOPER**	15
4	(7)	**JAMES STEWART**	4
5	(6)	**MARILYN MONROE**	2
6	(4)	**ALAN LADD**	3
7	(-)	**WILLIAM HOLDEN**	1
8	(5)	**BING CROSBY**	15
9	(-)	**JANE WYMAN**	1
10	(-)	**MARLON BRANDO**	1

1955

1	(4)	**JAMES STEWART**	5
2	(-)	**GRACE KELLY**	1
3	(1)	**JOHN WAYNE**	7
4	(7)	**WILLIAM HOLDEN**	2
5	(3)	**GARY COOPER**	16
6	(10)	**MARLON BRANDO**	2
7	(2)	**MARTIN & LEWIS**	5
8	(-)	**HUMPHREY BOGART**	8
9	(-)	**JUNE ALLYSON**	1
10	(-)	**CLARK GABLE**	16

1956

1	(4)	**WILLIAM HOLDEN**	3
2	(3)	**JOHN WAYNE**	8
3	(1)	**JAMES STEWART**	6
4	(-)	**BURT LANCASTER**	1
5	(-)	**GLENN FORD**	1
6	(7)	**MARTIN & LEWIS**	6
7	(5)	**GARY COOPER**	17
8	(-)	**MARILYN MONROE**	3
9	(-)	**KIM NOVAK**	1
10	(-)	**FRANK SINATRA**	1

1957

1	(-)	**ROCK HUDSON**	1
2	(2)	**JOHN WAYNE**	9
3	(-)	**PAT BOONE**	1
4	(-)	**ELVIS PRESLEY**	1
5	(10)	**FRANK SINATRA**	2
6	(7)	**GARY COOPER**	18
7	(1)	**WILLIAM HOLDEN**	4
8	(3)	**JAMES STEWART**	7
9	(-)	**JERRY LEWIS** (solo)	1
10	(-)	**YUL BRYNNER**	1

1958

1	(-)	**GLENN FORD**	2
2	(-)	**ELIZABETH TAYLOR**	1
3	(9)	**JERRY LEWIS**	2
4	(-)	**MARLON BRANDO**	3
5	(1)	**ROCK HUDSON**	2
6	(7)	**WILLIAM HOLDEN**	5
7	(-)	**BRIGITTE BARDOT**	1
8	(10)	**YUL BRYNNER**	2
9	(8)	**JAMES STEWART**	8
10	(5)	**FRANK SINATRA**	3

1959

1	(5)	**ROCK HUDSON**	3
2	(-)	**CARY GRANT**	4
3	(9)	**JAMES STEWART**	9
4	(-)	**DORIS DAY**	3
5	(-)	**DEBBIE REYNOLDS**	1
6	(1)	**GLENN FORD**	3
7	(10)	**FRANK SINATRA**	4
8	(-)	**JOHN WAYNE**	10
9	(3)	**JERRY LEWIS**	3
10	(-)	**SUSAN HAYWARD**	3

1960

1	(4)	**DORIS DAY**	4
2	(1)	**ROCK HUDSON**	4
3	(2)	**CARY GRANT**	5
4	(-)	**ELIZABETH TAYLOR**	2
5	(5)	**DEBBIE REYNOLDS**	2
6	(-)	**TONY CURTIS**	1
7	(-)	**SANDRA DEE**	1
8	(7)	**FRANK SINATRA**	5
9	(-)	**JACK LEMMON**	1
10	(8)	**JOHN WAYNE**	11

1961

1	(4)	**ELIZABETH TAYLOR**	3
2	(2)	**ROCK HUDSON**	5
3	(1)	**DORIS DAY**	5
4	(10)	**JOHN WAYNE**	12
5	(3)	**CARY GRANT**	6
6	(7)	**SANDRA DEE**	2
7	(-)	**JERRY LEWIS**	4
8	(-)	**WILLIAM HOLDEN**	6
9	(6)	**TONY CURTIS**	2
10	(-)	**ELVIS PRESLEY**	2

1962

1	(3)	**DORIS DAY**	6
2	(2)	**ROCK HUDSON**	6
3	(5)	**CARY GRANT**	7
4	(4)	**JOHN WAYNE**	13
5	(10)	**ELVIS PRESLEY**	3
6	(1)	**ELIZABETH TAYLOR**	4
7	(7)	**JERRY LEWIS**	5
8	(-)	**FRANK SINATRA**	6
9	(6)	**SANDRA DEE**	3
10	(-)	**BURT LANCASTER**	2

1963

1	(1)	**DORIS DAY**	7
2	(4)	**JOHN WAYNE**	14
3	(2)	**ROCK HUDSON**	7
4	(-)	**JACK LEMMON**	2
5	(3)	**CARY GRANT**	8
6	(6)	**ELIZABETH TAYLOR**	5
7	(5)	**ELVIS PRESLEY**	4
8	(9)	**SANDRA DEE**	4
9	(-)	**PAUL NEWMAN**	1
10	(7)	**JERRY LEWIS**	6

1964

1	(1)	**DORIS DAY**	8
2	(4)	**JACK LEMMON**	3
3	(3)	**ROCK HUDSON**	8
4	(2)	**JOHN WAYNE**	15
5	(5)	**CARY GRANT**	9
6	(7)	**ELVIS PRESLEY**	5
7	(-)	**SHIRLEY MacLAINE**	1
8	(-)	**ANN-MARGRET**	1
9	(9)	**PAUL NEWMAN**	2
10	(-)	**RICHARD BURTON**	1

1965

1	(-)	**SEAN CONNERY**	1
2	(4)	**JOHN WAYNE**	16
3	(1)	**DORIS DAY**	9
4	(-)	**JULIE ANDREWS**	1
5	(2)	**JACK LEMMON**	4
6	(6)	**ELVIS PRESLEY**	6
7	(5)	**CARY GRANT**	10
8	(-)	**JAMES STEWART**	10
9	(-)	**ELIZABETH TAYLOR**	6
10	(10)	**RICHARD BURTON**	2

1966

1	(4)	**JULIE ANDREWS**	2
2	(1)	**SEAN CONNERY**	2
3	(9)	**ELIZABETH TAYLOR**	7
4	(5)	**JACK LEMMON**	5
5	(10)	**RICHARD BURTON**	3
6	(7)	**CARY GRANT**	11
7	(2)	**JOHN WAYNE**	17
8	(3)	**DORIS DAY**	10
9	(-)	**PAUL NEWMAN**	3
10	(6)	**ELVIS PRESLEY**	7

1967

1	(1)	**JULIE ANDREWS**	3
2	(-)	**LEE MARVIN**	1
3	(9)	**PAUL NEWMAN**	4
4	(-)	**DEAN MARTIN**	1
5	(2)	**SEAN CONNERY**	3
6	(3)	**ELIZABETH TAYLOR**	8
7	(-)	**SIDNEY POITIER**	1
8	(7)	**JOHN WAYNE**	18
9	(5)	**RICHARD BURTON**	4
10	(-)	**STEVE McQUEEN**	1

Sean Connery

Sidney Poitier

Julie Andrews

1968

1	(7)	**SIDNEY POITIER**	2
2	(3)	**PAUL NEWMAN**	5
3	(1)	**JULIE ANDREWS**	4
4	(8)	**JOHN WAYNE**	19
5	(-)	**CLINT EASTWOOD**	1
6	(4)	**DEAN MARTIN**	2
7	(10)	**STEVE McQUEEN**	2
8	(-)	**JACK LEMMON**	6
9	(2)	**LEE MARVIN**	2
10	(6)	**ELIZABETH TAYLOR**	9

1969

1	(2)	**PAUL NEWMAN**	6
2	(4)	**JOHN WAYNE**	20
3	(7)	**STEVE McQUEEN**	3
4	(-)	**DUSTIN HOFFMAN**	1
5	(5)	**CLINT EASTWOOD**	2
6	(1)	**SIDNEY POITIER**	3
7	(9)	**LEE MARVIN**	3
8	(8)	**JACK LEMMON**	7
9	(-)	**KATHARINE HEPBURN**	1
10	(-)	**BARBRA STREISAND**	1

1970

1	(1)	**PAUL NEWMAN**	7
2	(5)	**CLINT EASTWOOD**	(3)
3	(3)	**STEVE McQUEEN**	4
4	(2)	**JOHN WAYNE**	21
5	(-)	**ELLIOTT GOULD**	1
6	(4)	**DUSTIN HOFFMAN**	2
7	(7)	**LEE MARVIN**	4
8	(8)	**JACK LEMMON**	8
9	(10)	**BARBRA STREISAND**	2
10	(-)	**WALTER MATTHAU**	1

1971

1	(4)	**JOHN WAYNE**	22
2	(2)	**CLINT EASTWOOD**	4
3	(1)	**PAUL NEWMAN**	8
4	(3)	**STEVE McQUEEN**	5
5	(-)	**GEORGE C SCOTT**	1
6	(6)	**DUSTIN HOFFMAN**	3
7	(10)	**WALTER MATTHAU**	2
8	(-)	**ALI MacGRAW**	1
9	(-)	**SEAN CONNERY**	4
10	(7)	**LEE MARVIN**	5

Robert Redford

1972

1	(2)	**CLINT EASTWOOD**	5
2	(5)	**GEORGE C SCOTT**	2
3	(-)	**GENE HACKMAN**	1
4	(1)	**JOHN WAYNE**	23
5	(-)	**BARBRA STREISAND**	3
6	(-)	**MARLON BRANDO**	4
7	(3)	**PAUL NEWMAN**	9
8	(4)	**STEVE McQUEEN**	6
9	(6)	**DUSTIN HOFFMAN**	4
10	(-)	**GOLDIE HAWN**	1

1973

1	(1)	**CLINT EASTWOOD**	6
2	(-)	**RYAN O'NEAL**	1
3	(8)	**STEVE McQUEEN**	7
4	(-)	**BURT REYNOLDS**	1
5	(-)	**ROBERT REDFORD**	1
6	(5)	**BARBRA STREISAND**	4
7	(7)	**PAUL NEWMAN**	10
8	(-)	**CHARLES BRONSON**	1
9	(4)	**JOHN WAYNE**	24
10	(6)	**MARLON BRANDO**	6

1974

1	(5)	**ROBERT REDFORD**	2
2	(1)	**CLINT EASTWOOD**	7
3	(7)	**PAUL NEWMAN**	11
4	(6)	**BARBRA STREISAND**	5
5	(3)	**STEVE McQUEEN**	8
6	(4)	**BURT REYNOLDS**	2
7	(8)	**CHARLES BRONSON**	2
8	(-)	**JACK NICHOLSON**	1
9	(-)	**AL PACINO**	1
10	(9)	**JOHN WAYNE**	25

1975

1	(1)	**ROBERT REDFORD**	3
2	(4)	**BARBARA STREISAND**	4
3	(9)	**AL PACINO**	2
4	(7)	**CHARLES BRONSON**	3
5	(3)	**PAUL NEWMAN**	12
6	(2)	**CLINT EASTWOOD**	8
7	(6)	**BURT REYNOLDS**	3
8	(-)	**WOODY ALLEN**	1
9	(5)	**STEVE McQUEEN**	9
10	(-)	**GENE HACKMAN**	2

1976

1	(1)	**ROBERT REDFORD**	(4)
2	(-)	**JACK NICHOLSON**	2
3	(-)	**DUSTIN HOFFMAN**	5
4	(6)	**CLINT EASTWOOD**	9
5	(-)	**MEL BROOKS**	1
6	(7)	**BURT REYNOLDS**	4
7	(3)	**AL PACINO**	3
8	(-)	**TATUM O'NEAL**	1
9	(8)	**WOODY ALLEN**	2
10	(4)	**CHARLES BRONSON**	4

1977

1	(-)	**SYLVESTER STALLONE**	1
2	(-)	**BARBRA STREISAND**	5
3	(4)	**CLINT EASTWOOD**	10
4	(6)	**BURT REYNOLDS**	6
5	(1)	**ROBERT REDFORD**	5
6	(9)	**WOODY ALLEN**	3
7	(5)	**MEL BROOKS**	2
8	(7)	**AL PACINO**	4
9	(-)	**DIANE KEATON**	1
10	(-)	**ROBERT DeNIRO**	1

1978

1	(4)	**BURT REYNOLDS**	7
2	(-)	**JOHN TRAVOLTA**	1
3	(-)	**RICHARD DREYFUSS**	1
4	(-)	**WARREN BEATTY**	1
5	(3)	**CLINT EASTWOOD**	11
6	(6)	**WOODY ALLEN**	4
7	(9)	**DIANE KEATON**	2
8	(-)	**JANE FONDA**	1
9	(-)	**PETER SELLERS**	1
10	(2)	**BARBRA STREISAND**	6

1979

1	(1)	**BURT REYNOLDS**	8
2	(3)	**CLINT EASTWOOD**	12
3	(8)	**JANE FONDA**	2
4	(6)	**WOODY ALLEN**	5
5	(10)	**BARBRA STREISAND**	7
6	(-)	**SYLVESTER STALLONE**	2
7	(2)	**JOHN TRAVOLTA**	2
8	(-)	**JILL CLAYBURGH**	1
9	(-)	**ROGER MOORE**	1
10	(-)	**MEL BROOKS**	3

1980

1	(1)	**BURT REYNOLDS**	9
2	(-)	**ROBERT REDFORD**	6
3	(2)	**CLINT EASTWOOD**	13
4	(3)	**JANE FONDA**	3
5	(-)	**DUSTIN HOFFMAN**	6
6	(7)	**JOHN TRAVOLTA**	3
7	(-)	**SALLY FIELD**	1
8	(-)	**SISSY SPACEK**	1
9	(5)	**BARBRA STREISAND**	8
10	(-)	**STEVE MARTIN**	1

It has already been pointed out that these listings favour artists who consistently turn out successful films, rather than those who appear in the occasional blockbuster. The frequency of their output has much to do with the high placings continually achieved in recent years by both Clint Eastwood and Burt Reynolds. People like Robert Redford, Dustin Hoffman and Sylvester Stallone, of comparable box office appeal, tend to move in and out of these listings, as they make fewer, though equally successful, films.

Figures for 1981 were not available as this book was being compiled, but undoubtedly will be by the time it is read. Reynolds and Eastwood will most certainly be in the Top Ten once again, together with Jane Fonda, Harrison Ford (a debut), and probably Dudley Moore, his namesake Roger, and Richard Pryor.

Joan Crawford

THE TOP TEN BOX OFFICE STARS OF EACH DECADE (1930s – 1970s)

Analysis of the Annual Quigley Poll Box Office top ten lists reveals the ten most popular box office stars of each decade. These are shown below, along with a listing of their most popular films released during that decade.

THE 1930s

1 **CLARK GABLE**
Notable films: 'Red Dust' (1932); 'It Happened One Night' (1934); 'Manhattan Melodrama' (1934); 'Mutiny on the Bounty' (1935); 'Call of the Wild' (1935); 'San Francisco' (1936); 'Too Hot to Handle' (1938); 'Gone With the Wind' (1939).

2 **SHIRLEY TEMPLE**
Notable films: 'Stand Up And Cheer' (1934); 'Little Miss Marker' (1934); 'Curly Top' (1935); 'Dimples' (1936); 'Wee Willie Winkie' (1937); 'Heidi' (1937); 'Rebecca of Sunnybrook Farm' (1938); 'The Little Princess' (1939).

3 **WILL ROGERS**
Notable films: 'A Connecticut Yankee' (1931); 'State Fair' (1933); 'Handy Andy' (1934); 'Judge Priest' (1934); 'Life Begins at Forty' (1935); 'Steamboat Round the Bend' (1935).

4 **JANET GAYNOR**
Notable films: 'The Man Who Came Back' (1930); 'Delicious' (1932); 'State Fair' (1933); 'Change Of Heart' (1934); 'A Star Is Born' (1937); 'The Young in Heart' (1938).

5 **JOAN CRAWFORD**
Notable films: 'Laughing Sinners' (1931); 'Grand Hotel' (1932); 'Rain' (1932); 'Dancing Lady' (1933); 'Forsaking All Others' (1935); 'The Gorgeous Hussy' (1936); 'The Last of Mrs Cheney' (1937); 'The Women' (1939).

6 **MARIE DRESSLER**
Notable films: 'Anna Christie' (1930); 'Min and Bill' (1930); 'Politics' (1931); 'Emma' (1932); 'Prosperity' (1932); 'Tugboat Annie' (1933); 'Dinner at Eight' (1933).

7 **WALLACE BEERY**
Notable films: 'Min and Bill' (1930); 'Hell Divers' (1932); 'Grand Hotel' (1932); 'The Champ' (1931); 'Dinner at Eight' (1933); 'Tugboat Annie' (1933); 'Treasure Island' (1934); 'China Seas' (1935); 'Slave Ship' (1937); 'Stand Up and Fight' (1939).

8 **FRED ASTAIRE & GINGER ROGERS**
Notable films: 'Flying Down to Rio' (1933); 'Roberta' (1935); 'Top Hat' (1935); 'Follow the Fleet' (1936); 'Swing Time' (1936); 'Shall We Dance?' (1937); 'Carefree' (1938); 'The Story of Vernon & Irene Castle' (1939).

9 **MICKEY ROONEY**
Notable films: 'A Midsummer Night's Dream' (1934); 'Ah Wilderness' (1935); 'Captains Courageous' (1937); 'A Family Affair' (1937); 'Judge Hardy's Children' (1938); 'Boys' Town' (1938); 'The Adventures of Huckleberry Finn' (1939); 'Babes in Arms' (1939).

10 **SPENCER TRACY**
Notable films: 'Disorderly Conduct' (1932); '20,000 Years in Sing Sing' (1932); 'The Power and the Glory' (1933); 'A Man's Castle' (1933); 'It's a Small World' (1935); 'San Francisco' (1936); 'Libeled Lady' (1936); 'Captains Courageous' (1937); 'Test Pilot' (1938); 'Boys' Town' (1938); 'Stanley and Livingstone' (1939).

Bing Crosby

Betty Grable

THE 1940s

1 **BING CROSBY**
   Notable films: 'The Road to Singapore' (1940); 'The Road to Zanzibar' (1941); 'The
   Birth of the Blues' (1941); 'Holiday Inn' (1942); 'The Road to Morocco' (1942);
   'Going My Way' (1944); 'Dixie' (1942); 'Here Come the Waves' (1945); 'The Bells of
   St Mary's' (1945); 'The Road to Rio' (1948); 'A Connecticut Yankee in King Arthur's
   Court' (1949).

2 **BOB HOPE**
   Notable films: The Road to Singapore' (1940); 'The Road to Zanzibar' (1941); 'My
   Favourite Blonde' (1942); 'The Road to Morocco' (1942); 'Let's Face It' (1943); 'The
   Princess and the Pirate' (1944); 'Monsieur Beaucaire' (1946); 'The Road to Rio'
   (1948); 'The Paleface' (1948); 'The Great Lover' (1949).

3 **GARY COOPER**
   Notable films: 'The Westerner' (1940); 'Meet John Doe' (1941); 'Sergeant York'
   (1941); 'For Whom the Bell Tolls' (1943); 'Along Came Jones' (1945);
   'Unconquered' (1947); 'The Fountainhead' (1949).

4 **BETTY GRABLE**
   Notable films: 'Tin Pan Alley' (1940); 'Moon Over Miami' (1941); 'I Wake Up
   Screaming' (1941); 'Coney Island' (1943); 'Sweet Rosie O'Grady' (1943); 'Diamond
   Horseshoe' (1945); 'Mother Wore Tights' (1947); 'When My Baby Smiles at Me'
   (1948).

5 **ABBOTT AND COSTELLO**
   Notable films: 'Hold That Ghost' (1941); 'In Society' (1944); 'The Naughty Nineties'
   (1945); 'The Time of Their Lives' (1946); '...Meet Frankenstein' (1948); '...Meet the
   Killers' (1949).

6 **CLARK GABLE**
   Notable films: 'Boom Town' (1940); 'Somewhere I'll Find You' (1941); 'The
   Hucksters' (1947); 'Homecoming' (1948); 'Command Decision' (1948).

7 **HUMPHREY BOGART**
   Notable films: 'High Sierra' (1941); 'The Maltese Falcon' (1941); 'Across the Pacific'
   (1942); 'Casablanca' (1942); 'Sahara' (1943); 'To Have and Have Not' (1944); 'The
   Big Sleep' (1946); 'The Treasure of the Sierra Madre' (1947); 'Key Largo' (1948).

8 **SPENCER TRACY**
Notable films: 'North West Passage' (1940); 'Boom Town' (1940); 'Dr Jekyll and Mr Hyde' (1941); 'Woman of the Year' (1942); 'Keeper of the Flame' (1943); 'The Seventh Cross' (1944); 'Without Love' (1945); 'State of the Union' (1948); 'Adam's Rib' (1949).

9 **MICKEY ROONEY**
Notable films: 'The Human Comedy' (1943); 'Girl Crazy' (1943); 'National Velvet' (1944); 'Summer Holiday' (1947).

10 **GREER GARSON**
Notable films: 'Blossoms in the dust' (1941); 'Mrs Miniver' (1942); 'Random Harvest' (1942); 'Madame Curie' (1943); 'Mrs Parkington' (1944); 'Adventure' (1945); 'That Forsyte Woman' (1949).

THE 1950s

1 **JOHN WAYNE**
Notable films: 'Flying Leathernecks' (1951); 'The Quiet Man' (1952); 'Hondo' (1953); 'The High and the Mighty' (1954); 'Sea Chase' (1955); 'The Conqueror' (1955); 'The Searchers' (1956); 'Rio Bravo' (1959); 'The Horse Soldiers' (1959).

2 **JAMES STEWART**
Notable films: 'Harvey' (1950); 'No Highway' (1951); 'The Greatest Show on Earth' (1951); 'The Glenn Miller Story' (1953); 'Rear Window' (1954); 'The Man From Laramie' (1955); 'The Man Who Knew Too Much' (1956); 'The Spirit of St Louis' (1957); 'Vertigo' (1958); 'Anatomy of a Murder' (1959).

3 **DEAN MARTIN & JERRY LEWIS**
Notable films: 'At War With the Army' (1951); 'That's My Boy' (1951); 'Sailor Beware' (1951); 'Jumping Jacks' (1952); 'The Stooge' (1952); 'Scared Stiff' (1953); 'The Caddy' (1953); 'Living It Up' (1954); 'Hollywood or Bust' (1956).

4 **GARY COOPER**
Notable films: 'Distant Drums' (1951); 'High Noon' (1952); 'Vera Cruz' (1954); 'Friendly Persuasion' (1956); 'Ten North Frederick' (1958); 'The Wreck of the Mary Deare' (1959).

5 **BING CROSBY**
Notable films: 'Here Comes the Groom' (1951); 'Just for You' (1952); 'The Road to Bali' (1952); 'Little Boy Lost' (1953); 'White Christmas' (1954); 'The Country Girl' (1954); 'High Society' (1956).

6 **WILLIAM HOLDEN**
Notable films: 'Sunset Boulevard' (1950); 'Born Yesterday' (1950); 'Stalag 17' (1953); 'The Moon Is Blue' (1953); 'Sabrina' (1954); 'The Country Girl' (1954); 'The Bridges at Toko-Ri' (1954); 'Love Is a Many Spendoured Thing' (1955); 'Picnic' (1955); 'The Proud and the Profane' (1956); 'The Bridge on the River Kwai' (1957); 'The Horse Soldiers' (1959).

7 **ROCK HUDSON**
Notable films: 'The Bend of the River' (1952); 'Magnificent Obsession' (1954); 'Giant' (1956); 'Written on the Wind' (1956); 'Tarnished Angels' (1957); 'A Farewell to Arms' (1957); 'Pillow Talk' (1959).

8 **BOB HOPE**
Notable films: 'Fancy Pants' (1950); 'Son of Paleface' (1952); 'The Road to Bali' (1952); 'That Certain Feeling' (1956); 'Alias Jesse James' (1959).

9 **GLENN FORD**
Notable films: 'Time Bomb' (1953); 'The Big Heat' (1953); 'The Blackboard Jungle' (1955); 'The Fastest Gun Alive' (1956); 'The Teahouse of the August Moon' (1956); '3.10 to Yuma' (1957); 'Don't Go Near the Water' (1957); 'The Sheepman' (1958).

10 **BETTY GRABLE**
Notable films: 'My Blue Heaven' (1950); 'Call Me Mister' (1951); 'How to Marry a Millionaire' (1953).

Kirk Douglas and Doris Day

THE 1960s

1 **JOHN WAYNE**
Notable films: 'North to Alaska' (1960); 'The Alamo' (1960); 'The Comancheros' (1961); 'The Man Who Shot Liberty Valance' (1962); 'Hatari' (1962); 'The Longest Day' (1962); 'How the West Was Won' (1963); 'The Greatest Story Ever Told' (1965); 'In Harm's Way' (1965); 'The Sons of Katie Elder' (1965); 'El Dorado' (1967); 'The War Wagon' (1967); 'The Green Berets' (1968); 'True Grit' (1969).

2 **DORIS DAY**
Notable films: 'Please Don't Eat the Daisies' (1960); 'Midnight Lace' (1960); 'Lover Come Back' (1962); 'That Touch of Mink' (1962); 'The Thrill of It All' (1963); 'Move Over Darling' (1963); 'Send Me No Flowers' (1964).

3 **CARY GRANT**
Notable films: 'The Grass Is Greener' (1960); 'That Touch of Mink' (1962); 'Charade' (1963); 'Father Goose' (1964); 'Walk, Don't Run' (1966).

4 **ROCK HUDSON**
Notable films: 'Come September' (1961); 'Man's Favourite Sport' (1964); 'Send Me No Flowers' (1964); 'Seconds' (1966); 'Ice Station Zebra' (1968).

5 **ELIZABETH TAYLOR**
Notable films: 'Butterfield 8' (1960); 'Cleopatra' (1960); 'The VIPs' (1963); 'The Sandpiper' (1965); 'Who's Afraid of Virginia Woolf?' (1966); 'The Taming of the Shrew' (1967).

6 **JACK LEMMON**
Notable films: 'The Apartment' (1960); 'The Wackiest Ship in the Army' (1960); 'Days of Wine and Roses' (1962); 'Irma La Douce' (1963); 'Good Neighbour Sam' (1964); 'How to Murder Your Wife' (1965); 'The Great Race' (1965); 'The Odd Couple' (1968); 'The April Fools' (1969); 'The Out-of-Towners' (1969).

7 JULIE ANDREWS
Notable films: 'Mary Poppins' (1964); 'The Americanization of Emily' (1964); 'The Sound of Music' (1965); 'Torn Curtain' (1966); 'Thoroughly Modern Millie' (1967); 'Star' (1968).

8 PAUL NEWMAN
Notable films: 'From the Terrace' (1960); 'Exodus' (1960); 'The Hustler' (1961); 'Sweet Bird of Youth' (1962); 'Hud' (1963); 'The Prize' (1963); 'What a Way to Go' (1964); 'Torn Curtain' (1966); 'Harper' (1966); 'Hombre' (1967); 'Cool Hand Luke' (1967); 'Winning' (1969); 'Butch Cassidy and the Sundance Kid' (1969).

9 SEAN CONNERY
Notable films: 'The Frightened City' (1960); 'The Longest Day' (1962); 'Dr. No' (1962); 'From Russia With Love' (1963); 'Woman of Straw' (1964); 'Marnie' (1964); 'Goldfinger' (1964); 'The Hill' (1965); 'Thunderball' (1965); 'You Only Live Twice' (1967).

10 ELVIS PRESLEY
Notable films: 'G.I. Blues' (1960); 'Flaming Star' (1960); 'Blue Hawaii' (1961); 'Follow That Dream' (1962); 'Viva Las Vegas' (1964).

Rock Hudson

Clint Eastwood

Burt Reynolds and Rachel Ward

THE 1970s

1 **CLINT EASTWOOD**
Notable films: 'Two Mules for Sister Sara' (1970); 'The Beguiled' (1971); 'Play Misty for Me' (1971); 'Dirty Harry' (1971); 'Joe Kidd' (1972); 'High Plains Drifter' (1973); 'Magnum Force' (1973); 'Thunderbolt and Lightfoot' (1974); 'The Outlaw Josey Wales' (1976); 'The Enforcer' (1976); 'The Gauntlet' (1977); 'Every Which Way But Loose' (1978); 'Escape from Alcatraz' (1979).

2 **BURT REYNOLDS**
Notable films: 'Deliverance' (1972); 'The Longest Yard' (1974); 'WW and the Dixie Dance Kings' (1975); 'Lucky Lady' (1976); 'Gator' (1976); 'Smokey and the Bandit' (1977); 'The End' (1978); 'Hooper' (1978); 'Starting Over' (1979).

3 **BARBRA STREISAND**
Notable films: 'The Owl and the Pussycat' (1970). 'What's Up, Doc?' (1972); 'The Way We Were' (1973); 'For Pete's Sake' (1974); 'Funny Lady' (1975); 'A Star Is Born' (1976); 'The Main Event' (1979).

4 **ROBERT REDFORD**
Notable films: 'Jeremiah Johnson' (1972); 'The Candidate' (1972); 'The Way We Were' (1973); 'The Sting' (1973); 'The Great Gatsby' (1974); 'The Great Waldo Pepper' (1975); 'Three Days of the Condor' (1975); 'All the President's Men' (1976); 'A Bridge Too Far' (1977); 'The Electric Horseman' (1979).

5 **PAUL NEWMAN**
Notable films: 'Judge Roy Bean' (1972); 'The Sting' (1973); 'The Towering Inferno' (1974); 'Buffalo Bill and the Indians' (1976); 'Slap Shot' (1977); 'Quintet' (1979).

6 **STEVE McQUEEN**
Notable films: 'The Reivers' (1970); 'Le Mans' (1971); 'The Getaway' (1972); 'Papillon' (1973); 'The Towering Inferno' (1974); 'An Enemy of the People' (1976).

7 **JOHN WAYNE**
Notable films: 'Chisum' (1970); 'Big Jake' (1971); 'The Cowboys' (1972); 'McQ' (1974); 'Rooster Cogburn' (1975); 'The Shootist' (1976).

8 **WOODY ALLEN**
Notable films: 'Bananas' (1971); 'Everything You Always Wanted to Know About Sex' (1972); 'Play It Again Sam' (1972); 'Sleeper' (1973); 'Love and Death' (1976); 'Annie Hall' (1977); 'Interiors' (1978); 'Manhattan' (1979).

9 DUSTIN HOFFMAN

Notable films: 'Little Big Man' (1970); 'Straw Dogs' (1972); 'Papillon' (1973); 'Lenny' (1974); 'All the President's Men' (1976); 'Marathon Man' (1976); 'Straight Time' (1978).

10 AL PACINO

Notable films: 'The Godfather' (1972); 'Serpico' (1973); 'The Godfather, Part II' (1974); 'Dog Day Afternoon' (1975); 'Bobby Deerfield' (1977).

It is interesting to note that the most popular star in each decade has to date always been male, although many female stars did top individual yearly lists. The ladies' total representation has, moreover, fallen off through the years — the 1930s list is almost equally balanced; but by the 1970s only Barbra Streisand made it into the Top Ten. It is conceivable that a few more years of consistent success by such recent top-rating stars as Diane Keaton, Jane Fonda and Sally Field could reverse this trend by the time the 1980s draw to a close.

Support for the musical side of the cinema, at its height prior to the growth of the post-war recording industry and the advent of TV variety shows, remained apparent up until the 60s, but again when we come to the last decade under review, Barbra Streisand is the only artist on the list to have gained her place through musical roles (and then only partially).

By contrast, the macho element — always strongly represented, but increasingly so as the years moved on — seemed to come to a peak during the 70s, with six of the decade's top box office stars regularly flexing their muscles as well as their talent on screen.

Finally, it should be noted that the grand-daddy macho of them all, John Wayne, was the only star whose Top Ten box office status spanned three decades, in two of which he was clearly the most popular artist on the screen.

Woody Allen

Barbara Streisand

Marlon Brando

THE TOP 100 MONEY MAKING FILMS OF ALL TIME

Every year America's weekly entertainment business bible 'Variety' compiles an updated list of all-time box office successes. This listing is based upon figures totalled from distributors' rental receipts throughout the North American continent (that is, the USA and Canada). It should be noted, however, that these figures do not represent box office ticket sale grosses, or — more importantly — total audience attendances. The majority of positions on the listing are for films released during the 1970s and 1980s, (84% of the top 100 in total); this is largely a reflection of the fact that the figures are based on prices, not on audiences. Monetary inflation, covering the 45-year period from 'Snow White and the Seven Dwarfs' (the earliest film in the top 100) to 'Raiders of the Lost Ark' (one of the most recent), has exerted a considerable and obvious bias in favour of recent films with their much larger rental fees.

It might be noted in this connection that 'Raiders' $90 million earnings by the end of 1981 is less than four times as much as 'Snow White's' current total of almost $27 million. Assuming a 400% inflation rate in rental fees over the period to be a conservative estimate, it could be argued that, comparatively, the more recent film has not yet come near the earnings ratio of the earlier one. On the other hand, it has not had a 45-year earning period.

A staggeringly successful double — 'Star Wars' and 'The Empire Strikes Back' — produced by George Lucas and Gary Kurtz, occupy the top two places in the list, and have, to date, grossed $319,347,000. Harrison Ford's performance in these two films, together with his starring role in 'Raiders of the Lost Ark', means that his cinematic contribution has grossed in excess of $400 million.

It is a widely held view that 'Gone With the Wind', placed at No. 12, remains the film seen by the most people. This view, bearing in mind the adjustment which needs to be made to the receipt figures due to inflation, would seem to be borne out by the statistics. Further analysis of the top 100 reveals 11 films which are sequels to earlier ones, including the two Pink Panther movies of the 70s, made more than 10 years after the original. The most successful sequel of all — 'The Empire Strikes Back' — lies just one position behind its forerunner.

'Snow White and the Seven Dwarfs' trails 'The Jungle Book' by two places as the most successful cartoon ever, while the mixed live/animation 'Mary Poppins' at No. 34 is Walt Disney's biggest-grossing picture. 'Animal House' at No. 14 is the most successful comedy to date, while 'Grease', which has grossed nearly $100 million, clearly leads 'The Sound of Music' on the musical front. Two of the Top Ten — 'Jaws' and 'The Exorcist' — could probably be classed as horror films, while science fiction themes (in the guise of the two 'Star Wars' films, 'Superman', and 'Raiders of the Lost Ark' as a borderline case) clearly dominate the really big money-spinners.

(The listing shows title and director, the total reported North American box office receipts up to the end of 1981, and the year of release.)

1   **STAR WARS** *(George Lucas)*
    $185,138,000 (1977)
2   **THE EMPIRE STRIKES BACK** *(Irvin Kershner)*
    $134,209,000 (1980)
3   **JAWS** *(Steven Spielberg)*
    $133,435,000 (1975)
4   **GREASE** *(Randal Kleiser)*
    $96,300,000 (1978)
5   **RAIDERS OF THE LOST ARK** *(Steven Spielberg)*
    $90,434,000 (1981)
6   **THE EXORCIST** *(William Friedkin)*
    $88,500,000 (1973)
7   **THE GODFATHER** *(Francis Ford Coppola)*
    $86,275,000 (1972)
8   **SUPERMAN: THE MOVIE** *(Richard Donner)*
    $82,500,000 (1979)
9   **THE SOUND OF MUSIC** *(Robert Wise)*
    $79,748,000 (1965)
10 **THE STING** *(George Roy Hill)*
    $78,963,000 (1973)
11 **CLOSE ENCOUNTERS OF THE THIRD KIND** *(Steven Spielberg)*
    $77,000,000 (1977)

Harrison Ford

Vivien Leigh and Clark Gable

12 **GONE WITH THE WIND** *(Victor Fleming)*
$76,700,000 (1939)

13 **SATURDAY NIGHT FEVER** *(John Badham)*
$74,100,000 (1977)

14 **NATIONAL LAMPOON'S ANIMAL HOUSE** *(John Landis)*
$74,000,000 (1978)

15 **SUPERMAN 2** *(Dick Lester)*
$64,000,000 (1981)

16 **KRAMER VS. KRAMER** *(Robert Benton)*
$61,734,000 (1979)

17 **SMOKEY AND THE BANDIT** *(Hal Needham)*
$61,055,000 (1977)

18 **ONE FLEW OVER THE CUCKOO'S NEST** *(Milos Forman)*
$59,166,036 (1975)

19 **STIR CRAZY** *(Sidney Poitier)*
$58,408,000 (1980)

20 **NINE TO FIVE** *(Colin Higgins)*
$57,850,000 (1980)

21 **STAR TREK: THE MOTION PICTURE** *(Robert Wise)*
$56,000,000 (1979)

22 **ROCKY** *(John G Avildsen)*
$55,892,428 (1976)

23 **AMERICAN GRAFFITI** *(George Lucas)*
$55,886,000 (1973)

117

Dustin Hoffman and Anne Bancroft

Roy Scheider, Steven Laft and Steven Spielburg

24 **JAWS II** *(Jeannot Szwarc)*
$55,608,000 (1978)

25 **EVERY WHICH WAY BUT LOOSE** *(James Fargo)*
$51,800,000 (1978)

26 **LOVE STORY** *(Arthur Hiller)*
$50,000,000 (1970)

27 **THE TOWERING INFERNO** *(John Guillermin)*
$50,000,000 (1974)

28 **HEAVEN CAN WAIT** *(Warren Beatty/Buck Henry)*
$49,400,000 (1978)

29 **THE GRADUATE** *(Mike Nichols)*
$49,078,000 (1968)

30 **DR ZHIVAGO** *(David Lean)*
$46,550,000 (1965)

31 **BUTCH CASSIDY AND THE SUNDANCE KID** *(George Roy Hill)*
$46,039,000 (1969)

32 **AIRPORT** *(George Seaton)*
$45,300,000 (1970)

33 **BLAZING SADDLES** *(Mel Brooks)*
$45,200,000 (1974)

34 **MARY POPPINS** *(Robert Stevenson)*
$45,000,000 (1964)

35 **ROCKY II** *(Sylvester Stallone)*
$43,049,274 (1979)

36 **THE TEN COMMANDMENTS** *(Cecil B De Mille)*
$43,000,000 (1956)

36 **THE JERK** *(Carl Reiner)*
$43,000,000 (1979)

38 **THE POSEIDON ADVENTURE** *(Ronald Neame)*
$42,000,000 (1972)

39 **THE GOODBYE GIRL** *(Herbert Ross)*
$41,700,000 (1977)

40 **AIRPLANE** *(Jim Abrahams/David Zucker/Jerry Zucker)*
$40,610,000 (1980)

41 **FIDDLER ON THE ROOF** *(Norman Jewison)*
$40,498,669 (1971)

42 **ALIEN** *(Ridley Scott)*
$39,847,000 (1979)

43 **STRIPES** *(Ivan Reitman)*
$39,514,000 (1981)

44 **ANY WHICH WAY YOU CAN** *(Buddy Van Horn)*
$39,500,000 (1980)

45 **YOUNG FRANKENSTEIN** *(Mel Brooks)*
$38,823,000 (1974)

46 **COAL MINER'S DAUGHTER** *(Michael Apted)*
$38,500,000 (1980)

47 **SMOKEY AND THE BANDIT II** *(Hal Needham)*
$37,600,000 (1980)

48 **APOCALYPSE NOW** *(Francis Ford Coppola)*
$37,268,881 (1979)

49 **A STAR IS BORN** *(Frank Pierson)*
$37,100,000 (1976)

50 **ARTHUR** *(Steve Gordon)*
$37,000,000 (1981)

51 **KING KONG** *(John Guillermin)*
$36,915,000 (1976)

52 **M*A*S*H** *(Robert Altman)*
$36,720,000 (1970)

53 **BEN HUR** *(William Wyler)*
$36,650,000 (1959)

54 **EARTHQUAKE** *(Mark Robson)*
$36,250,000 (1974)

55 **'10'** *(Blake Edwards)*
$36,000,000 (1979)

56 **THE CANNONBALL RUN** *(Hal Needham)*
$35,378,000 (1981)

57 **THE AMITYVILLE HORROR** *(Stuart Rosenberg)*
$35,000,000 (1979)

58 **HOOPER** *(Hal Needham)*
$34,900,000 (1978)

59 **PRIVATE BENJAMIN** *(Howard Zieff)*
$34,000,000 (1980)

60 **MOONRAKER** *(Lewis Gilbert)*
$33,934,074 (1979)

61 **BILLY JACK** *(Tom Laughlin)*
$32,500,000 (1971)

62 **THE BLUES BROTHERS** *(John Landis)*
$32,200,000 (1980)

63 **THE MUPPET MOVIE** *(James Frawley)*
$32,000,000 (1979)

64 **OH GOD** *(Carl Reiner)*
$31,440,000 (1977)

65 **THE DEEP** *(Peter Yates)*
$31,300,000 (1977)

66 **THE ELECTRIC HORSEMAN** *(Sydney Pollack)*
$31,116,000 (1979)

67 **THE SHINING** *(Stanley Kubrick)*
$30,800,000 (1980)

68 **THE GODFATHER, PART II** *(Francis Ford Coppola)*
$30,673,000 (1974)

69 **THE DEER HUNTER** *(Michael Cimino)*
$30,425,000 (1978)

70 **THE BLUE LAGOON** *(Randal Kleiser)*
$30,327,000 (1980)

71 **SILVER STREAK** *(Arthur Hiller)*
$30,018,000 (1976)

72 **ALL THE PRESIDENT'S MEN** *(Alan J Pakula)*
$30,000,000 (1976)

73 **CALIFORNIA SUITE** *(Herbert Ross)*
$29,200,000 (1978)

74 **THE OMEN** *(Richard Donner)*
$28,544,000 (1976)

75 **THUNDERBALL** *(Terence Young)*
$28,530,000 (1965)

76 **UP IN SMOKE** *(Lou Adler)*
$28,300,000 (1978)

77 **PATTON** *(Franklin J Schaffner)*
$28,100,000 (1970)

78 **WHAT'S UP DOC** *(Peter Bogdanovich)*
$28,000,000 (1972)

79 **FOUL PLAY** *(Colin Higgins)*
$27,500,000 (1978)

80 **THE JUNGLE BOOK** *(animated)*
$27,300,000 (1967)

81 **THE FOUR SEASONS** *(Alan Alda)*
$26,800,000 (1981)

82 **SNOW WHITE AND THE SEVEN DWARFS** *(animated)*
$26,750,000 (1937)

83 **FUNNY GIRL** *(William Wyler)*
$26,325,000 (1968)

84 **THE FRENCH CONNECTION** *(William Friedkin)*
$26,315,000 (1971)

85 **THE MAIN EVENT** *(Howard Zieff)*
$26,300,000 (1979)

86 **THE CHINA SYNDROME** *(James Bridges)*
$26,073,700 (1979)

87 **CLEOPATRA** *(Joseph L Mankiewicz)*
$26,000,000 (1962)

88 **AIRPORT 1975** *(Jack Smight)*
$25,805,000 (1974)

89 **GUESS WHO'S COMING TO DINNER?** *(Stanley Kramer)*
$25,500,000 (1968)

Snow White and the Seven Dwarfs

The Lady and the Tramp

90 **FOR YOUR EYES ONLY** *(John Glen)*
    $25,439,479 (1981)

91 **THE BLACK HOLE** *(Gary Nelson)*
    $25,425,000 (1979)

92 **RETURN OF THE PINK PANTHER** *(Blake Edwards)*
    $25,390,617 (1975)

93 **LADY AND THE TRAMP** *(animated)*
    $25,150,000 (1955)

94 **THE WAY WE WERE** *(Sydney Pollack)*
    $25,000,000 (1973)

95 **THE REVENGE OF THE PINK PANTHER** *(Blake Edwards)*
    $25,000,000 (1978)

96 **THE BAD NEWS BEARS** *(Michael Ritchie)*
    $24,888,000 (1976)

97 **POPEYE** *(Robert Altman)*
    $24,568,541 (1980)

98 **THE SPY WHO LOVED ME** *(Lewis Gilbert)*
    $24,322,345 (1977)

99 **2001: A SPACE ODYSSEY** *(Stanley Kubrick)*
    $24,100,000 (1968)

100 **THE ENFORCER** *(James Fargo)*
    $24,000,000 (1976)

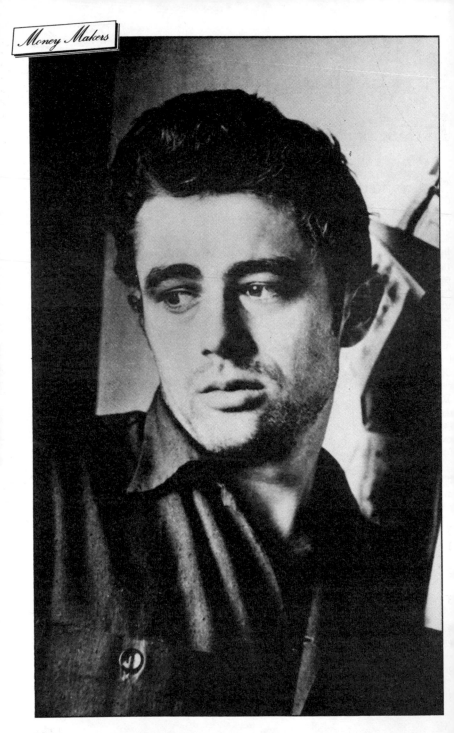

THE TOP MONEY MAKING FILMS OF EACH YEAR 1947–1981

In 1947, the annual rental earnings for the year's most successful films were first reported in 'Variety'; prior to this date, annual listings were given in alphabetical order, with no indication either of rank or the figures involved. The figures in the first 12 of these lists (that is, prior to 1959) are rounded approximations which were taken from the studios' extrapolations of a film's likely final revenue, based upon its degree of activity in the early period of release.

In later listings, the figures represent actual earned revenue at the cut-off point at the end of the year. Whilst generally more accurate, the later system does tend to favour films released in the early part of the year; releases from the final quarter of a year are now often included with the listings of the following year, for this reason. Many films obviously have a final revenue (as indicated in the all-time top 100) in excess of their initial year-end total, due to extended runs, reissues, and the continued showing of the film into the following year. Conversely, there are films in the earlier listings here which ultimately failed to quite achieve the projected total of earnings they were allocated — 'The Robe', and 'Peyton Place', for instance.

The listings which follow include the film titles in rank order, and the earning figures in dollars, as published. The figures up to 1979 are those which appeared in the 'Variety' year-end listings; those for 1980 and 1981 refer to total gross receipts shown in the 1981-end all-time listing.

1947

1 **THE BEST YEARS OF OUR LIVES** ($11,500,000)
2 **DUEL IN THE SUN** ($10,750,000)
3 **THE JOLSON STORY** ($8,000,000)

1948

1 **THE ROAD TO RIO** ($4,500,000)
2 **EASTER PARADE** ($4,200,000)
3 **RED RIVER** ($4,150,000)

1949

1 **JOLSON SINGS AGAIN** ($5,500,000)
2 **PINKY** ($4,200,000)
3 **I WAS A MALE WAR BRIDE** ($4,100,000)

1950

1 **SAMSON AND DELILAH** ($11,000,000)
2 **BATTLEGROUND** ($4,550,000)
3 **KING SOLOMON'S MINES** ($4,400,000)

The Robe

1951
1 **DAVID AND BATHSHEBA**
($7,000,000)
2 **SHOWBOAT**
($5,200,000)
3 **AN AMERICAN IN PARIS**
($4,500,000)
3 **THE GREAT CARUSO**
($4,500,000)

1952
1 **THE GREATEST SHOW
ON EARTH** ($12,000,000)
2 **QUO VADIS**
($10,500,000)
3 **IVANHOE**
($7,000,000)

1953
1 **THE ROBE**
($20,000,000)
2 **FROM HERE TO ETERNITY**
(12,500,000)
3 **SHANE**
($8,000,000)

1954
1 **WHITE CHRISTMAS**
($12,000,000)
2 **THE CAINE MUTINY**
($8,700,000)
3 **THE GLENN MILLER STORY**
($7,000,000)

1955
1 **CINERAMA HOLIDAY**
($10,000,000)
2 **MISTER ROBERTS**
($8,500,000)
3 **BATTLE CRY**
($8,000,000)
3 **20,000 LEAGUES UNDER
THE SEA** ($8,000,000)

1956
1 **GUYS AND DOLLS**
($9,000,000)
2 **THE KING AND I**
(8,500,000)
3 **TRAPEZE**
($7,500,000)

1957
1 **THE TEN COMMANDMENTS**
($18,500,000)
2 **AROUND THE WORLD IN 80 DAYS** ($16,200,000)
3 **GIANT**
($12,000,000)

1958
1 **THE BRIDGE ON THE RIVER KWAI** ($18,000,000)
2 **PEYTON PLACE**
($12,000,000)
3 **SAYONARA**
($10,500,000)

1959
1 **AUNTIE MAME**
($8,800,000)
2 **SHAGGY DOG**
($7,800,000)
3 **SOME LIKE IT HOT**
($7,000,000)

1960
1 **BEN HUR**
($17,300,000)
2 **PSYCHO**
($8,500,000)
3 **OPERATION PETTICOAT**
($6,800,000)
4 **SUDDENLY LAST SUMMER**
($5,500,000)
5 **ON THE BEACH**
($5,300,000)

1961
1 **THE GUNS OF NAVARONE**
($8,600,000)
2 **THE ABSENT-MINDED PROFESSOR** ($8,200,000)
3 **THE PARENT TRAP**
($8,000,000)
4 **SWISS FAMILY ROBINSON**
($7,500,000)
5 **EXODUS** ($7,350,000)

The Ten Commandments

Alec Guinness

David Niven

Julie Andrews

1962

1 **SPARTACUS**
($13,500,000)
2 **WEST SIDE STORY**
($11,000,000)
3 **LOVER COME BACK**
($8,500,000)
3 **THAT TOUCH OF MINK**
($8,500,000)
5 **EL CID**
($8,000,000)
5 **THE MUSIC MAN**
($8,000,000)

1963

1 **CLEOPATRA**
($15,700,000)
2 **THE LONGEST DAY**
($12,750,000)
3 **IRMA LA DOUCE**
($9,250,000)
4 **LAWRENCE OF ARABIA**
($9,000,000)
5 **HOW THE WEST WAS WON**
($8,000,000)

Sean Connery

1964

1 **THE CARPETBAGGERS** ($13,000,000)

2 **IT'S A MAD, MAD, MAD, MAD WORLD** ($10,000,000)

3 **THE UNSINKABLE MOLLY BROWN** ($7,500,000)

4 **CHARADE** ($6,150,000)

5 **THE CARDINAL** ($5,275,000)

1965

1 **MARY POPPINS** ($28,500,000)

2 **THE SOUND OF MUSIC** ($20,000,000)

3 **GOLDFINGER** ($19,700,000)

4 **MY FAIR LADY** ($19,000,000)

5 **WHAT'S NEW, PUSSYCAT?** ($7,150,000)

1966

1 **THUNDERBALL** ($26,000,000)

2 **DOCTOR ZHIVAGO** ($15,000,000)

3 **WHO'S AFRAID OF VIRGINIA WOOLF?** ($10,300,000)

4 **THAT DARN CAT** ($9,200,000)

5 **THE RUSSIANS ARE COMING, THE RUSSIANS ARE COMING** ($7,750,000)

1967

1 **THE DIRTY DOZEN** ($18,200,000)

2 **YOU ONLY LIVE TWICE** ($16,300,000)

3 **CASINO ROYALE** ($10,200,000)

4 **A MAN FOR ALL SEASONS** ($9,250,000)

5 **THOROUGHLY MODERN MILLIE** ($8,500,000)

1968

1 **THE GRADUATE**
($39,000,000)
2 **GUESS WHO'S COMING TO DINNER?**
($25,100,000)
3 **GONE WITH THE WIND**
($23,000,000)
4 **VALLEY OF THE DOLLS**
($20,000,000)
5 **THE ODD COUPLE**
($18,500,000)

1969

1 **THE LOVE BUG**
($17,000,000)
2 **FUNNY GIRL**
($16,500,000)
3 **BULLITT**
($16,400,000)
4 **BUTCH CASSIDY AND THE SUNDANCE KID**
($15,000,000)
5 **ROMEO AND JULIET**
($14,500,000)

1970

1 **AIRPORT**
($37,650,000)
2 **M*A*S*H**
($22,000,000)
3 **PATTON**
($21,000,000)
4 **BOB AND CAROL AND TED AND ALICE**
($13,900,000)
5 **WOODSTOCK**
($13,500,000)
6 **HELLO DOLLY!**
($13,000,000)
7 **CACTUS FLOWER**
($11,300,000)
8 **CATCH 22**
($9,250,000)
9 **ON HER MAJESTY'S SECRET SERVICE**
($9,000,000)
10 **THE REIVERS**
($8,000,000)

1971

1 **LOVE STORY**
($50,000,000)
2 **LITTLE BIG MAN**
($15,000,000)
3 **SUMMER OF '42**
($14,000,000)
4 **RYAN'S DAUGHTER**
($13,400,000)
5 **THE OWL AND THE PUSSYCAT**
($11,500,000)
6 **THE ARISTOCATS**
($10,100,000)
7 **CARNAL KNOWLEDGE**
($9,347,000)
8 **WILLARD**
($8,200,000)
9= **THE ANDROMEDA STRAIN**
($7,500,000)
9= **BIG JAKE**
($7,500,000)

1972

1 **THE GODFATHER**
($81,500,000)
2 **FIDDLER ON THE ROOF**
($25,100,000)
3 **DIAMONDS ARE FOREVER**
($21,000,000)
4 **WHAT'S UP, DOC?**
($17,000,000)
5 **DIRTY HARRY**
($16,000,000)
6 **THE LAST PICTURE SHOW**
($12,750,000)
7 **A CLOCKWORK ORANGE**
($12,000,000)
8 **CABARET**
($10,885,000)
9 **THE HOSPITAL**
($9,000,000)
10 **EVERYTHING YOU ALWAYS WANTED TO KNOW ABOUT SEX — BUT WERE AFRAID TO ASK**
($8,500,000)

The Jungle Book

The Jungle Book

1973

1 **THE POSEIDON ADVENTURE**
($40,000,000)
2 **DELIVERANCE**
($18,000,000)
3 **THE GETAWAY**
($17,500,000)
4 **LIVE AND LET DIE**
($15,500,000)
5 **PAPER MOON**
($13,000,000)
6 **LAST TANGO IN PARIS**
($12,625,000)
7 **THE SOUND OF MUSIC**
(reissue) ($11,000,000)
8 **JESUS CHRIST SUPERSTAR**
($10,800,000)
9 **THE WORLD'S GREATEST ATHLETE**
($10,600,000)
10 **AMERICAN GRAFFITI**
($10,300,000)

1975

1 **JAWS**
($102,650,000)
2 **THE TOWERING INFERNO**
($55,000,000)
3 **BENJI**
($30,800,000)
4 **YOUNG FRANKENSTEIN**
($30,000,000)
5 **THE GODFATHER, PART II**
($28,900,000)
6 **SHAMPOO**
($22,000,000)
7 **FUNNY LADY**
($20,000,000)
8 **MURDER ON THE ORIENT EXPRESS**
($17,800,000)
9 **THE RETURN OF THE PINK PANTHER**
($17,000,000)
10 **TOMMY**
($16,000,000)

1974

1 **THE STING**
($68,450,000)
2 **THE EXORCIST**
($66,300,000)
3 **PAPILLON**
($19,750,000)
4 **MAGNUM FORCE**
($18,300,000)
5 **HERBIE RIDES AGAIN**
($17,500,000)
6 **BLAZING SADDLES**
($16,500,000)
7 **THE TRIAL OF BILLY JACK**
($15,000,000)
8 **THE GREAT GATSBY**
($14,200,000)
9 **SERPICO**
($14,100,000)
10 **BUTCH CASSIDY AND THE SUNDANCE KID**
($13,820,000)

1976

1 **ONE FLEW OVER THE CUCKOO'S NEST**
($56,500,000)
2 **ALL THE PRESIDENT'S MEN**
($29,000,000)
3 **THE OMEN**
($27,851,000)
4 **THE BAD NEWS BEARS**
($26,266,517)
5 **SILENT MOVIE**
($20,311,000)
6 **MIDWAY**
($20,300,000)
7 **DOG DAY AFTERNOON**
($19,800,000)
8 **MURDER BY DEATH**
($18,800,000)
9 **JAWS** (reissue)
($16,077,000)
10 **BLAZING SADDLES** (reissue)
($13,850,000)

Francis Ford Coppola

1977

1 **STAR WARS**
($127,000,000)

2 **ROCKY**
($54,000,000)

3 **SMOKEY AND THE BANDIT**
($39,744,000)

4 **A STAR IS BORN**
($37,100,000)

5 **KING KONG**
($35,851,283)

6 **THE DEEP**
($31,000,000)

7 **SILVER STREAK**
($27,100,000)

8 **THE ENFORCER**
($24,000,000)

9 **CLOSE ENCOUNTERS OF THE THIRD KIND**
($23,000,000)

9 **IN SEARCH OF NOAH'S ARK**
($23,000,000)

1978

1 **GREASE**
($83,091,000)

2 **CLOSE ENCOUNTERS OF THE THIRD KIND**
($54,000,000)

3 **NATIONAL LAMPOON'S ANIMAL HOUSE**
($52,368,000)

4 **JAWS 2**
($49,299,000)

5 **HEAVEN CAN WAIT**
($42,517,000)

6 **THE GOODBYE GIRL**
($41,000,000)

7 **STAR WARS** (reissue)
($38,375,000)

8 **HOOPER**
($31,500,000)

9 **FOUL PLAY**
($25,065,000)

10 **THE REVENGE OF THE PINK PANTHER**
($25,000,000)

1979

1 **SUPERMAN: THE MOVIE**
  ($81,000,000)
2 **EVERY WHICH WAY BUT LOOSE**
  ($48,000,000)
3 **ROCKY II**
  ($43,049,274)
4 **ALIEN**
  ($40,086,573)
5 **THE AMITYVILLE HORROR**
  ($35,000,000)
5 **STAR TREK: THE MOTION PICTURE**
  ($35,000,000)
7 **MOONRAKER**
  ($33,934,074)
8 **THE MUPPET MOVIE**
  ($32,000,000)
9 **CALIFORNIA SUITE**
  ($29,200,000)
10 **THE DEER HUNTER**
  ($26,927,000)

1981

1 **RAIDERS OF THE LOST ARK**
  ($90,434,000)
2 **SUPERMAN II**
  ($64,000,000)
3 **STIR CRAZY**
  ($58,408,000)
4 **NINE TO FIVE**
  ($57,850,000)
5 **STRIPES**
  ($39,514,000)
6 **ANY WHICH WAY YOU CAN**
  ($39,500,000)
7 **ARTHUR**
  ($37,000,000)
8 **THE CANNONBALL RUN**
  ($35,378,000)
9 **THE FOUR SEASONS**
  ($26,800,000)
10 **FOR YOUR EYES ONLY**
  ($25,439,479)

1980

1 **THE EMPIRE STRIKES BACK**
  ($120,059,000)
2 **KRAMER VS. KRAMER**
  ($61,734,000)
3 **THE JERK**
  ($43,000,000)
4 **AIRPLANE**
  ($40,610,000)
5 **COAL MINER'S DAUGHTER**
  ($38,500,000)
6 **SMOKEY AND THE BANDIT II**
  ($37,600,000)
7 **PRIVATE BENJAMIN**
  ($34,000,000)
8 **THE BLUES BROTHERS**
  ($32,200,000)
9 **THE ELECTRIC HORSEMAN**
  ($31,116,000)
10 **THE SHINING**
  ($30,800,000)

There is little discernible pattern in these annual listings, although it is interesting to note here that — despite the trend of decreasing cinema audiences — the blockbuster film still draws the crowds in similar numbers to earlier years. The gap between the top films of each year and the rest is now wider than it has ever been, and the middle ground becomes harder and harder to fill each year. This can be little comfort to the majority of film makers, particularly as the full impact of video has yet to be felt.

To date, only three films — 'Jaws', 'Star Wars' and 'The Empire Strikes Back' — have hit a nine figure amount with their first year's grossings. However, it seems quite likely that with the trend towards colossal, widely appealing spectaculars like these three, 'Raiders of the Lost Ark' and 'Superman' — and with the constant spiral of inflation — a gross of over $100 million could become the norm during the 1980s for the most successful film of the year.

Alfred Hitchcock

THE TOP 20 MONEY MAKING FILMS OF EACH DECADE

Since the cinema rental fees which make up the top 100 films, as reported by 'Variety', are a reflection of distributors' receipts rather than audience attendance, the problem of monetary inflation over the years is (as already mentioned) a distorting factor in favour of the more recent films on the list. However, by extracting the most financially successful films of each decade, it is possible to pinpoint the big earners of earlier years, by measuring them only against their near contemporaries; these films might otherwise have their success obscured by later productions. It ought still to be remembered that inflation does not only operate in 10-yearly leaps, so that even within the lists which follow, there will be an earning bias towards films which appeared near the end of a decade. The listings show the year of release beside each title.

PRIOR TO 1940

As rental earnings were not reported for the annual 'Variety' compilations prior to 1947, it is difficult to assess the financial success of many films released prior to that date, particularly those from the 1930s and before. There are, of course, exceptions; for many years 'Gone With the Wind' and 'Snow White and the Seven Dwarfs' were the top-grossing films of all time, and their distributors would quote regularly updated figures to remind people of this fact (both these films still figure in the all-time Top 100 list.)

Only a comparatively small number of other big earners from these early years have had figures subsequently quoted, so that although the list below covers two decades rather than one, the titles shown on it are only those for which figures are available. It is possible that other films, such as 'It Happened One Night' and 'All Quiet on the Western Front', should be here, particularly those from the 30s. In order, however, to keep the listing free from speculative elements, only the nine following titles are eligible:-

1   **GONE WITH THE WIND** (1939)
2   **SNOW WHITE AND THE SEVEN DWARFS** (1937)
3   **THE BIG PARADE** (1925)
4   **THE BIRTH OF A NATION** (1915)
5   **KING KONG** (1933)
6   **THE WIZARD OF OZ** (1939)
7   **BEN HUR** (1926)
8   **SAN FRANCISCO** (1936)
9   **THE SINGING FOOL** (1928)

Fantasia

Snow White and the Seven Dwarfs

The Best Years of Our Lives

THE 1940s

Most of the really large earning films of the 1940s, including many whose figures were not initially published, have had overall totals announced in later years. It should be remembered, with regard to Walt Disney's apparent domination of the decade, that Disney films are reissued regularly on a cyclic basis (usually to further substantial success); those shown here are probably as popular today with young filmgoers as they ever were.

1 **SONG OF THE SOUTH** (1946)
2 **PINOCCHIO** (1940)
3 **FANTASIA** (1940)
4 **BAMBI** (1942)
5 **CINDERELLA** (1949)
6 **SAMSON AND DELILAH** (1949)
7 **THE BEST YEARS OF OUR LIVES** (1946)
8 **DUEL IN THE SUN** (1946)
9 **THE BELLS OF ST MARY'S** (1945)
10 **THE JOLSON STORY** (1946)
11 **FOR WHOM THE BELL TOLLS** (1943)
12 **GOING MY WAY** (1944)
13 **WELCOME STRANGER** (1947)
14 **LIFE WITH FATHER** (1947)
15 **BLUE SKIES** (1946)
16 **VALLEY OF DECISION** (1945)
17 **MRS MINIVER** (1942)
18 **LEAVE HER TO HEAVEN** (1945)
19 **THE EGG AND I** (1947)
20 **UNCONQUERED** (1947)

Ben Hur

THE 1950s

By the 1950s, the annual reporting and tabulation of rental earnings was well-established, and while not every film has had its total earnings officially updated from the time of original release, most of the figures used for determining this Top 20 ranking are those up to the end of 1981. Once again, some of the Walt Disney titles have had reissues and further successful runs, so benefitting their final totals.

1   **THE TEN COMMANDMENTS** (1956)
2   **BEN HUR** (1959)
3   **LADY AND THE TRAMP** (1955)
4   **AROUND THE WORLD IN 80 DAYS** (1956)
5   **THE ROBE** (1953)
6   **SOUTH PACIFIC** (1958)
7   **THE BRIDGE ON THE RIVER KWAI** (1957)
8   **PETER PAN** (1953)
9   **THE SLEEPING BEAUTY** (1959)
10 **THIS IS CINERAMA** (1952)
11 **THE GREATEST SHOW ON EARTH** (1952)
12 **GIANT** (1956)
13 **QUO VADIS** (1951)
14 **THE SEVEN WONDERS OF THE WORLD** (1956)
15 **THE SHAGGY DOG** (1959)
16 **FROM HERE TO ETERNITY** (1953)
17 **WHITE CHRISTMAS** (1954)
18 **CINERAMA HOLIDAY** (1955)
19 **PEYTON PLACE** (1958)
20 **20,000 LEAGUES UNDER THE SEA** (1954)

THE 1960s

In the mid 60s, 'The Sound of Music' overtook 'Gone With the Wind' as the biggest dollar-earning film of all time, although it was certainly true to say that inflation was taking a hand by now; moreover, rental fees can be assumed to have at least doubled between 1939 and 1965. 'Gone With the Wind' was reissued during the 60s, however, and the earnings it made during that period would obviously have been at the same comparatively inflated rate.

1   **THE SOUND OF MUSIC** (1965)
2   **THE GRADUATE** (1968)
3   **DR ZHIVAGO** (1965)
4   **BUTCH CASSIDY AND THE SUNDANCE KID** (1969)
5   **MARY POPPINS** (1964)
6   **THUNDERBALL** (1965)
7   **THE JUNGLE BOOK** (1967)
8   **FUNNY GIRL** (1968)
9   **CLEOPATRA** (1962)
10 **GUESS WHO'S COMING TO DINNER?** (1968)
11 **2001: A SPACE ODYSSEY** (1968)
12 **THE LOVE BUG** (1969)
13 **GOLDFINGER** (1964)
14 **101 DALMATIONS** (1961)
15 **BONNIE AND CLYDE** (1967)
16 **IT'S A MAD, MAD, MAD, MAD WORLD** (1963)
17 **MIDNIGHT COWBOY** (1969)
18 **THE DIRTY DOZEN** (1967)
19 **VALLEY OF THE DOLLS** (1967)
20 **THE ODD COUPLE** (1968)

Mary Poppins

THE 1970s

The mid and late 70s ushered in the megabuck earning age: seven of the current 10 all-time biggest-grossing films were made during this decade. However, the fact that two of the remaining Top Ten places have already been taken by films released during the 80s suggests that even some of these films may be pushed down to less significant placings by the end of the current decade.

1 **STAR WARS** (1977)
2 **JAWS** (1975)
3 **GREASE** (1978)
4 **THE EXORCIST** (1973)
5 **THE GODFATHER** (1972)
6 **SUPERMAN: THE MOVIE** (1979)
7 **THE STING** (1973)
8 **CLOSE ENCOUNTERS OF THE THIRD KIND** (1977)
9 **SATURDAY NIGHT FEVER** (1977)
10 **NATIONAL LAMPOON'S ANIMAL HOUSE** (1978)
11 **SMOKEY AND THE BANDIT** (1977)
12 **ONE FLEW OVER THE CUCKOO'S NEST** (1975)
13 **STAR TREK: THE MOTION PICTURE** (1979)
14 **ROCKY** (1976)
15 **AMERICAN GRAFFITI** (1973)
16 **JAWS II** (1978)
17 **EVERY WHICH WAY BUT LOOSE** (1978)
18 **LOVE STORY** (1970)
19 **THE TOWERING INFERNO** (1975)
20 **HEAVEN CAN WAIT** (1978)

THE 1980s TO DATE

The following are the biggest-grossing films released during 1980 and 1981. The list will obviously be considerably different by the time the 1980s are complete.

1 **THE EMPIRE STRIKES BACK** (1980)
2 **RAIDERS OF THE LOST ARK** (1981)
3 **SUPERMAN II** (1981)
4 **KRAMER VS. KRAMER** (1980)
5 **STIR CRAZY** (1980)
6 **NINE TO FIVE** (1980)
7 **AIRPLANE** (1980)
8 **STRIPES** (1981)
9 **ANY WHICH WAY YOU CAN** (1980)
10 **COAL MINER'S DAUGHTER** (1980)
11 **SMOKEY AND THE BANDIT II** (1980)

12 **ARTHUR** (1981)
13 **THE CANNONBALL RUN** (1981)
14 **PRIVATE BENJAMIN** (1980)
15 **THE BLUES BROTHERS** (1980)
16 **THE SHINING** (1980)
17 **THE BLUE LAGOON** (1980)
18 **THE FOUR SEASONS** (1981)
19 **FOR YOUR EYES ONLY** (1981)
20 **POPEYE** (1980)

Marilyn Monroe
146

MONEY MAKING FILMS OF THE MAJOR COMPANIES

Throughout most of Hollywood's history, the lion's share of film production and distribution has belonged to nine major companies. One of these, RKO (Radio-Keith-Orpheum), closed in the late 1950s, having foundered after huge earlier successes such as 'Cimarron', 'King Kong', 'Citizen Kane' and 'The Best Years of Our Lives'. The other majors continue, although MGM has recently merged with United Artists, and Warner and Columbia now actually share combined Hollywood studio facilities.

The listings which follow pinpoint the 10 most financially successful films of each company.

Universal City
c. 1921-1922/
*Carl Laemmle with
Harry Carey,
Eddy Lyons,
Frank Mago,
Priscilla Dean,
Virginia Faire,
Yvette Mitchell*

UNIVERSAL

Formed in 1912, Universal has had one of the most consistently successful Hollywood histories, beginning with the films of Valentino and continuing into the 30s with 'All Quiet on the Western Front' and the famous Dracula/Frankenstein horror cycle showcasing the likes of Karloff and Lugosi. This success rate has persisted right up to the present day, and inevitably Universal's Top Ten grossing films are all products of the 1970s and 80s.

1   **JAWS** (1975)
2   **THE STING** (1973)
3   **NATIONAL LAMPOON'S ANIMAL HOUSE** (1978)
4   **SMOKEY AND THE BANDIT** (1977)
5   **AMERICAN GRAFFITI** (1973)
6   **JAWS II** (1978)
7   **AIRPORT** (1970)
8   **THE JERK** (1979)
9   **COAL MINER'S DAUGHTER** (1980)
10 **SMOKEY AND THE BANDIT II** (1980)

United Artists/*Fairbanks, Korda, Pickford, Chaplin*

UNITED ARTISTS

United Artists was formed in 1919 by Mary Pickford, Douglas Fairbanks, D.W. Griffith and Charlie Chaplin, with the intent of establishing a company which would place the interests of artists above those of businessmen. All the founders made early films through the company, but there were many later changes of structure and ownership that reflected the mixed fortunes of the next three decades. The company's tradition of independent deals and productions bolstered its success as this trend developed in Hollywood, and UA finally hit the big time in the 1960s, with films like 'Tom Jones' and 'West Side Story' and then particularly the James Bond and Pink Panther series. Its biggest grosser, 'One Flew Over the Cuckoo's Nest', was, in the best United Artists tradition, made with an independent production company, Fantasy Films.

1 **ONE FLEW OVER THE CUCKOO'S NEST** (1975)
2 **ROCKY** (1976)
3 **THE GRADUATE** (1968)
4 **ROCKY II** (1979)
5 **FIDDLER ON THE ROOF** (1971)
6 **APOCALYPSE NOW** (1979)
7 **MOONRAKER** (1979)
8 **THUNDERBALL** (1965)
9 **FOR YOUR EYES ONLY** (1981)
10 **THE RETURN OF THE PINK PANTHER** (1975)

WARNER BROS

The Brothers Warner (Jack, Sam, Harry and Albert) founded their production company in 1922 and, with the launch of 'The Jazz Singer' in 1927, leapt into a dominant role in sound film development. The 1930s and 40s were studded with the company's successful gangster dramas and Busby Berkeley musicals, and in later years they maintained consistent commercial success. The top Ten grossers are therefore once again all recent productions.

Jack L Warner

1   **THE EXORCIST** (1973)
2   **SUPERMAN** (1978)
3   **SUPERMAN II** (1981)
4   **EVERY WHICH WAY BUT LOOSE** (1978)
5   **THE TOWERING INFERNO** (1975 — co-production with 20th Century Fox)
6   **BLAZING SADDLES** (1974)
7   **THE GOODBYE GIRL** (1977)
8   **ANY WHICH WAY YOU CAN** (1980)
9   **A STAR IS BORN** (1976)
10   **ARTHUR** (1981)

149

COLUMBIA

Columbia started up in 1924 under the guidance of Harry Cohn, a producer of shorts turned industry mogul, who guided the company autocratically for the next 30-odd years. Success arrived in the 30s with 'It Happened One Night' and other popular features by Frank Capra and Howard Hawks, while the push into the major league came in the 50s with films such as 'On the Waterfront', 'From Here to Eternity' and 'The Bridge on the River Kwai'.

The post-Cohn years of the 60s produced several acclaimed films like 'Lawrence of Arabia', 'Oliver!' and 'Easy Rider', but fortunes nose-dived soon afterwards and the company was forced to restructure. The recovery came in the second half of the 70s, spearheaded by the incredible success of 'Close Encounters of the Third Kind'.

1 **CLOSE ENCOUNTERS OF THE THIRD KIND** (1977)
2 **KRAMER VS. KRAMER** (1979)
3 **STIR CRAZY** (1980)
4 **STRIPES** (1981)
5 **THE DEEP** (1977)
6 **THE ELECTRIC HORSEMAN** (1979)
7 **THE BLUE LAGOON** (1980)
8 **CALIFORNIA SUITE** (1978)
9 **FUNNY GIRL** (1968)
10 **THE CHINA SYNDROME** (1979)

MGM

MGM was formed in 1924 by Marcus Loew, whose company, Loew's Inc., combined the resources of Metro Pictures Corporation, the Goldwyn Picture Company, and Louis B Mayer Pictures, under the umbrella of Metro-Goldwyn-Mayer. Loew died in 1927, and Mayer took MGM to huge success through the 30s, thanks to such films as 'Grand Hotel', 'The Great Ziegfeld' and 'Gone With the Wind', and stars like Clark Gable, Joan Crawford and Greta Garbo.

The 1930s was effectively MGM's golden age, for succeeding decades tended to see fluctuation between large successes and equally major lossmakers, and the decline became quite pronounced during the 60s despite the box office achievements of 'Doctor Zhivago' and '2001: A Space Odyssey', for instance. The company pared its activities considerably during the 70s, when it handed its distribution over to United Artists; this has more recently been followed by a complete merger with UA.

1 **GONE WITH THE WIND** (1939)
2 **DOCTOR ZHIVAGO** (1965)
3 **BEN HUR** (1959)
4 **2001: A SPACE ODYSSEY** (1968)
5 **THE DIRTY DOZEN** (1967)
6 **CLASH OF THE TITANS** (1981)
7 **RYAN'S DAUGHTER** (1970)
8 **COMA** (1978)
9 **NETWORK** (1976)
10 **THE CHAMP** (1979)

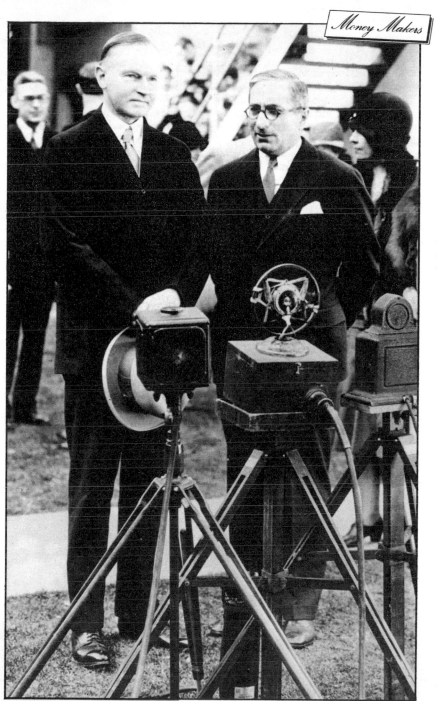

Louis B Mayer and President Coolidge

151

RKO

RKO, as mentioned earlier, was the first of the Hollywood majors to shut up shop, in 1958. Formed exactly 30 years earlier, Radio-Keith-Orpheum was the result of a merger between the fledgling RCA corporation, American Pathe, and the Keith, Albee and Orpheum cinema chain — masterminded by the entrepreneur Joseph P Kennedy (father of John, Bobby and Edward), who departed soon after.

RKO moved into high gear in the 1930s, thanks to the success of 'King Kong', the Western 'Cimarron', and the musical partnership of Fred Astaire and Ginger Rogers. RKO's distribution arm also handled the Walt Disney releases until Disney started his own Buena Vista distribution company.

The 1940s were highlighted by Orson Welles' 'Citizen Kane', Alfred Hitchcock's 'Notorious', and William Wyler's 'The Best Years of Our Lives'. However, in the early 1950s, under the control of Howard Hughes, internal problems and a dearth of successful productions led to eventual closure.

David Selznick

1	**THE BEST YEARS OF OUR LIVES** (1946)
2	**THE BELLS OF ST MARY'S** (1945)
3	**HANS CHRISTIAN ANDERSEN** (1952)
4	**THE OUTLAW** (1943)
5	**KING KONG** (1933)
6	**NOTORIOUS** (1946)
7	**THE BACHELOR AND THE BOBBYSOXER** (1947)
8	**THE CONQUEROR** (1955)
9	**JOAN OF ARC** (1948)
10	**THE KID FROM BROOKLYN** (1946)

WALT DISNEY

Formed in 1927 by the man whose name the company bears, the Disney studio has always occupied a unique role in the film world, being founded on animation rather than live action films, and sticking firmly to their policy of providing family entertainment. The best Disney films, notably the animated features, seem timeless because of their universality of appeal and the undatable fantasy element at their heart. For this reason, the company's policy of periodically recycling its films for new generations of audience has never failed to pay off.

Disney's initial success came from his animated shorts starring Mickey Mouse and the other members of this famous cartoon comedy menagerie, but his first feature length cartoon 'Snow White and the Seven Dwarfs' in 1937 — which almost bankrupted the company during its production — was a huge box office grosser and remains so even by modern standards.

Of the 10 films in this listing, six are full animations, two feature live action, and two — 'Mary Poppins' and 'Song of the South' — mix the two mediums.

Walt Disney

1	**MARY POPPINS** (1964)
2	**THE JUNGLE BOOK** (1967)
3	**SNOW WHITE AND THE SEVEN DWARFS** (1937)
4	**THE BLACK HOLE** (1979)
5	**LADY AND THE TRAMP** (1955)
6	**THE LOVE BUG** (1969)
7	**101 DALMATIONS** (1961)
8	**SONG OF THE SOUTH** (1946)
9	**PINOCCHIO** (1940)
10	**FANTASIA** (1940)

PARAMOUNT

Paramount Pictures emerged in 1935 from the ashes of Paramount Publix, a company which had been run for almost 20 years by Adolph Zukor. It had enjoyed tremendous early success with Mary Pickford and films like Cecil B De Mille's first version of 'The Ten Commandments', but had gone bankrupt in 1932. The reorganised company found success again with the Crosby films and the 'Road to' series, and maintained a consistent profile through the 40s, 50s and most of the 60s. In its first years under the current (since 1966) owner, the Gulf and Western group, the company foundered somewhat, but 1970 brought a huge renaissance with 'Love Story', and a regular stream of blockbusters followed from then on.

1   **GREASE** (1978)
2   **RAIDERS OF THE LOST ARK** (1981)
3   **THE GODFATHER** (1972)
4   **SATURDAY NIGHT FEVER** (1977)
5   **STAR TREK: THE MOTION PICTURE** (1979)
6   **LOVE STORY** (1970)
7   **HEAVEN CAN WAIT** (1978)
8   **THE TEN COMMANDMENTS** (1956)
9   **AIRPLANE** (1980)
10 **KING KONG** (1976)

Adolph Zukor and Mary Pickford

Harry F. Zanuck

20th CENTURY FOX

This company was formed in 1935 from a merger of Fox Film Company, and 20th Century Pictures, run by Darryl F Zanuck and Joseph Schenck. It settled into a consistent run with films featuring Shirley Temple, Tyrone Power and Betty Grable through the 40s, and moved into the 50s with stars like Gregory Peck and the newly-discovered Marilyn Monroe. Fox pioneered the wide screen Cinemascope process, and first used it to huge success in 'The Robe' in 1953. The 60s alternated between staggering successes such as 'The Sound of Music' and financial disasters like 'Cleopatra'; however, since 'M*A*S*H' in 1970, a string of spectacular winners have followed, including the two all-time box office champions of the 'Star Wars' saga.

1   **STAR WARS** (1977)
2   **THE EMPIRE STRIKES BACK** (1980)
3   **THE SOUND OF MUSIC** (1965)
4   **NINE TO FIVE** (1980)
5   **THE TOWERING INFERNO** (1975 — a co-production with Warner Bros.)
6   **BUTCH CASSIDY AND THE SUNDANCE KID** (1969)
7   **THE POSEIDON ADVENTURE** (1972)
8   **ALIEN** (1979)
9   **YOUNG FRANKENSTEIN** (1975)
10 **M*A*S*H** (1970)

Leslie Howard and Wendy Hiller

Trevor Howard

MONEY MAKING FILMS IN BRITAIN

The UK, with a considerably smaller (and fast-contracting) film exhibiting industry than that of the North American continent, plays a fairly insignificant role in the generation of revenue from films — a quite separate fact from the country's proven prowess at actually making them. Worldwide profits on a successful movie released internationally are generally anticipated to roughly equal those from the USA/Canadian release. Of this 50% world share, Britain's slice is miniscule, and this in itself is the reason why the UK's indigenous movie industry cannot be self-sufficient. It is unable to recoup its costs from exhibition in the British Isles only, but must seek to achieve its profit in the USA and elsewhere.

This state of affairs, coupled with the lack of a tradition of movie statistics, makes it impossible to present a comprehensive UK coverage. There are, however, some supplementary facts available which tend to highlight, if anything, a somewhat parochial attitude towards film production; details of the most successful domestic productions on the home market are given prominence, over those of the most successfully exhibited films per se. With the decline of the British industry, and the virtual extinction of productions which are British in every aspect, the emphasis today falls on the increasingly familiar phenomenon of films which may be American in terms of finance, stars, and possibly even subject matter, but which happen to be made in British studios.

The following list is a summary of those films which, since the Second World War, have been the most financially successful British productions at the home box office; several of the titles are recognisable as having found transatlantic success as well. The list shows directors and stars; figures for earnings are not available, but they would of course be miniscule in comparison with those achieved in America.

THE BIGGEST ANNUAL UK MONEY MAKING FILMS IN THE HOME MARKET, 1946–1981

(The listing shows year, title, director (bracketed) and main stars.)

1946 **THE WICKED LADY** (*Leslie Arliss*)
Margaret Lockwood, James Mason
1947 **THE COURTNEYS OF CURZON STREET** (*Herbert Wilcox*)
Anna Neagle, Michael Wilding
1948 **SPRING IN PARK LANE** (*Herbert Wilcox*)
Anna Neagle, Michael Wilding
1949 **THE THIRD MAN** (*Carol Reed*)
Joseph Cotten, Orson Welles, Trevor Howard

1950 **THE BLUE LAMP** *(Basil Dearden)*
Jack Warner, Jimmy Hanley, Dirk Bogarde

1951 **LAUGHTER IN PARADISE** *(Mario Zampi)*
Alastair Sim, Joyce Grenfell

1952 **WHERE NO VULTURES FLY** *(Harry Watt)*
Anthony Steel, Dinah Sheridan

1953 **THE CRUEL SEA** *(Charles Frend)*
Jack Hawkins, Donald Sinden, Stanley Baker

1954 **DOCTOR IN THE HOUSE** *(Ralph Thomas)*
Dirk Bogarde, Kenneth More

1955 **THE DAM BUSTERS** *(Michael Anderson)*
Michael Redgrave, Richard Todd

1956 **REACH FOR THE SKY** *(Lewis Gilbert)*
Kenneth More, Muriel Pavlow

1957 **DOCTOR AT LARGE** *(Ralph Thomas)*
Dirk Bogarde, Leslie Phillips

1958 **THE BRIDGE ON THE RIVER KWAI** *(David Lean)*
Alec Guinness, Jack Hawkins, William Holden

1959 **CARRY ON NURSE** *(Gerald Thomas)*
Kenneth Williams, Charles Hawtrey, etc.

1960 **DOCTOR IN LOVE** *(Ralph Thomas)*
Michael Craig

1961 **THE SWISS FAMILY ROBINSON** *(Ken Annakin)*
John Mills, Dorothy McGuire

1962 **THE YOUNG ONES** *(Sidney J Furie)*
Cliff Richard, Carole Gray, Robert Morley

1963 **FROM RUSSIA WITH LOVE** *(Terence Young)*
Sean Connery, Daniela Bianchi

1964 **GOLDFINGER** *(Guy Hamilton)*
Sean Connery, Honor Blackman, Gert Frobe

1965 **HELP!** *(Dick Lester)*
John Lennon, Paul McCartney, George Harrison, Ringo Starr, Leo McKern, Eleanor Bron

1966 **THUNDERBALL** *(Terence Young)*
Sean Connery, Adolfo Celi, Claudine Auger

1967 **YOU ONLY LIVE TWICE** *(Lewis Gilbert)*
Sean Connery, Tetsuro Tamba

1968 **UP THE JUNCTION** *(Peter Collinson)*
Suzy Kendall, Denis Waterman

1969 **OLIVER!** *(Carol Reed)*
Mark Lester, Oliver Reed, Ron Moody, Jack Wild

1970 **BATTLE OF BRITAIN** *(Guy Hamilton)*
Laurence Olivier, Michael Caine, Christopher Plummer, Robert Shaw

1971 **ON THE BUSES** *(Harry Booth)*
Reg Varney, Doris Hare, Anna Karen

1972 **DIAMONDS ARE FOREVER** *(Guy Hamilton)*
Sean Connery, Jill St John, Charles Gray

1973 **LIVE AND LET DIE** *(Guy Hamilton)*
Roger Moore, Yaphet Kotto, Jane Seymour

Money Makers

1974 CONFESSIONS OF A WINDOW CLEANER *(Val Guest)*
Robin Askwith

1975 THE MAN WITH THE GOLDEN GUN *(Guy Hamilton)*
Roger Moore, Christopher Lee, Britt Ekland

1976 THE RETURN OF THE PINK PANTHER *(Blake Edwards)*
Peter Sellers, Christopher Plummer, Catherine Schell

1977 THE SPY WHO LOVED ME *(Lewis Gilbert)*
Roger Moore, Barbara Bach, Curt Jurgens

1978 THE REVENGE OF THE PINK PANTHER *(Blake Edwards)*
Peter Sellers, Herbert Lom, Dyan Cannon

1979 MOONRAKER *(Lewis Gilbert)*
Roger Moore, Lois Chiles, Michel Lonsdale

1980 MONTY PYTHON'S LIFE OF BRIAN *(Terry Gilliam)*
John Cleese, Graham Chapman, Eric Idle, Michael Palin, Terry Jones, Terry Gilliam

1981 SUPERMAN II *(Dick Lester)*
Christopher Reeve, Gene Hackman, Margot Kidder
and also:
FOR YOUR EYES ONLY *(John Glen)*
Roger Moore

Humphrey Bogart

WHO GETS PAID THE MOST? — SOME MOVIE STAR SALARIES

It is a well known fact that film actors receive, by the standards of ordinary mortals, a lot of money for their efforts upon the screen. It should not be supposed, though, that every performer is (or was) regarded as equally payworthy; it is also surprising to discover that several latter-day box office champions worked for comparative peanuts at earlier stages in their careers.

The first list below, a fairly random sample, indicates annual salaries of several studio contracted players.

HUMPHREY BOGART — $39,000 from Fox (early 1930s)
BETTE DAVIS — $15,600 from Universal (early 1930s)
JAMES CAGNEY — $20,800 from Warner Bros (1930)
KATHARINE HEPBURN — $188,916 from MGM (1941)
SPENCER TRACY — $233,461 from MGM (1941)
JUDY GARLAND — $89,666 from MGM (1942)
BOB HOPE — $204,166 from Paramount (1941)
CARY GRANT — $93,750 from RKO (1939)
JOAN CRAWFORD — $194,615 from MGM (1943)
KIM NOVAK — $4,200 from Columbia (1955)

With the decline of the studio contract system, most stars were paid purely on a film by film basis — again, extremely variably with a multitude of factors affecting the size of the deal. Here are six particularly stingy ones.

CLINT EASTWOOD — $15,000 for 'A Fistful of Dollars' (1964)
DUSTIN HOFFMAN — $17,000 for 'The Graduate' (1967)
RUDOLPH VALENTINO — $5 per day while working on 'Alimony' (1918)
KIM NOVAK — $13,000 for 'Jeanne Eagels' (1957)
PAUL NEWMAN — $17,500 for each Warner Bros film (mid 1950s)
STEVE McQUEEN — $19 per day as an extra on 'Somebody Up There Likes Me' (1956)

And here are a few deals of the kind which must make stardom almost worth the hassle:

GEORGE C SCOTT — $1,000,000 plus a percentage of profits, for 'The Hindenburg' (1975)
STEVE McQUEEN — $1,000,000 for 'Bullitt' (1968)
ROBERT REDFORD — $2,000,000 for 'A Bridge Too Far' (1977)
JACK NICHOLSON — $1,250,000 plus 10% of gross receipts after $12,500,000, for 'The Missouri Breaks' (1976)

PAUL NEWMAN — $1,000,000 plus 10% (rising to 15% after break even) of gross receipts for *'The Towering Inferno'* (1974)

DUSTIN HOFFMAN — $425,000 for *'John and Mary'* (1969)

RICHARD BURTON — $1,000,000 plus a percentage of profits, for *'Anne of the Thousand Days'* (1970)

JULIE ANDREWS — $700,000 for *'Hawaii'* (1966)

JACQUELINE BISSET — $500,000 for *'Who Is Killing the Great Chefs of Europe?'* (1978)

SEAN CONNERY — $1,200,000 for *'Diamonds Are Forever'* (1971)

CLINT EASTWOOD — $400,000 plus 25% of net profits, for *'Hang 'Em High'* (1968)

MARLON BRANDO — $2,250,000 for *'Superman'* (1978)

The sheer unreality of the last fee quoted (which seems to be the highest ever per film payment to one individual) is brought home when it is realised that Brando, although he got top billing, only played a supporting character role in *'Superman'*. Christopher Reeve, who played the title role, got $250,000.

MONEY DOWN THE DRAIN: FILMS WITH NOTABLY DISASTROUS PROFIT-TO-COST RATIOS

The film industry trade magazine 'Variety' estimates that the average film needs to make 1.4 times its production costs in rental profits in order to actually break even, once things like promotion expenses and distributors' percentages are taken into account. This may not sound too difficult an achievement, and in fact films which adhere to a fairly modest budget, and then manage to capture the fancy of the movie-going audience to a reasonable degree, generally manage to justify their making in financial terms.

Obviously, the bigger the budget involved, the greater the risk of not earning back the investment. Some films are deliberately made as calculated risks: *'Close Encounters of the Third Kind'*, for instance, *had* to be one of the big financial hits of modern times just to break even on its colossal costs, but the producers were confident that the subject and the quality of the film, the reputation of director Spielberg, and the interest created by the publicity, would combine to make a winner. They were right, and the movie has to date grossed nearly $83,000,000 — against its $21,000,000 cost. However, when it comes down to it, the film itself has got to be right. Not just the director's reputation or a corporate confidence in the subject matter will do...as *'Heaven's Gate'*, the ultimate accountant's nightmare, has recently proved.

Isabelle Huppert and Kris Kristofferson

The listing below details some notable examples of films that 'failed'. There are undoubted surprises, as some of the films did in fact do very well at the box office. 'Cleopatra', for example, grossed $26,000,000 in North America, which puts it into the all-time Top 100 earners. Fine, if the film had cost $15,000,000 to make; unfortunately, it set 20th Century Fox back $44,000,000.

HEAVEN'S GATE (1980)
Cost: $36,000,000 — earnings to date: $1,500,000 —
loss to date: $34,500,000

RAISE THE TITANIC (1980)
Cost: $36,000,000 — earnings to date: $6,800,000 —
loss to date: $29,200,000

WATERLOO (1969)
Cost: $25,000,000 — earnings to date: $1,400,000 —
loss to date: $23,600,000

DARLING LILI (1970)
Cost: $22,000,000 — earnings to date: $3,300,000 —
loss to date: $18,700,000

Pot-pourri

163

THE FALL OF THE ROMAN EMPIRE (1964)
Cost: $20,000,000 — earnings to date: $1,900,000 —
loss to date: $18,100,000
CLEOPATRA (1962)
Cost: $44,000,000 — earnings to date: $26,000,000 —
loss to date: $18,000,000
HURRICANE (1979)
Cost: $22,000,000 — earnings to date: $4,900,000 —
loss to date: $17,100,000
HONKY TONK FREEWAY (1981)
Cost: $24,000,000 — earnings to date: $500,000 —
loss to date: $23,500,000
LEGEND OF THE LONE RANGER (1980)
Cost: $20,000,000 — earnings to date: $6,900,000 —
loss to date: $13,100,000
MUTINY ON THE BOUNTY (1962)
Cost: $20,000,000 — earnings to date: $9,800,000 —
loss to date: $10,200,000
THE GREATEST STORY EVER TOLD (1965)
Cost: $20,000,000 — earnings to date: $6,900,000 —
loss to date: $13,100,000
MOHAMMAD, MESSENGER OF GOD (1976)
Cost: $17,000,000 — earnings to date: $2,000,000 —
loss to date: $15,000,000
METEOR (1979)
Cost: $20,000,000 — earnings to date: $6,000,000 —
loss to date: $14,000,000
SORCERER (1977)
Cost: $22,000,000 — earnings to date: $5,900,000 —
loss to date: $16,100,000
THE WIZ (1978)
Cost: $24,000,000 — earnings to date: $13,600,000 —
loss to date: $10,400,000
DR DOLITTLE (1967)
Cost: $20,000,000 — earnings to date: $6,200,000 —
loss to date: $13,800,000
THE BATTLE OF BRITAIN (1969)
Cost: $12,000,000 — earnings to date: $2,000,000 —
loss to date: $10,000,000
TORA! TORA! TORA! (1970)
Cost: $25,000,000 — earnings to date: $14,500,000 —
loss to date $10,500,000
STAR! (1968)
Cost: $15,000,000 — earnings to date: $4,200,000 —
loss to date: $10,800,000
THE ISLAND (1980)
Cost: $22,000,000 — earnings to date: $9,600,000 —
loss to date: $12,400,000

FILMS MADE IN 3 – D

The 3-D cinema process began in 1915, with a series of experimental short films. The audience had to wear glasses with a red and a green lens to create the illusion of depth on the screen. The first 3-D feature film was *'Power of Love'* in 1922, and the first sound production in the process was an Italian film titled *'Nozze Vagabonde'* in 1936. These and other examples were all fairly isolated experiments, however, and none of them particularly successful.

A sudden boom in 3-D came in the early 50s in the USA, when the process was dusted off and lauded as a new major step in movie technology (as were other more enduring developments like Cinemascope, at around the same time). Approximately 50 3-D films were made in 1953-4, after which the flood dried up very quickly. This was partly because of the abysmal quality of most of the films, whose plots were generally bogged down with gimmicky effects which allowed objects to be pushed, pointed or thrown 'out' of the screen at the audience. There were also the practical inconveniences of issuing red and green specs to the audience, and converting cinema projection booths to make them suitable for the necessary dual-projection process.

However, 3-D wouldn't lie down. *'The Bubble'* appeared in 1967, *'The Four Dimensions of Greta'* and a couple of other soft porn offerings in the early 70s, and occasional films of a mostly exploitative nature since. *'Parasite'* and *'Comin' at Ya'* were released in 1972 — one a gory horror film, and the other an almost equally bloody spaghetti Western.

After the initial boom, most of the films made for 3-D were reprinted in 'flat' form, which is of course the way some of them have turned up on TV at later dates. Some of the best-remembered titles in the process are the following:

BWANA DEVIL
EYES OF HELL
IT CAME FROM OUTER SPACE
HOUSE OF WAX
KISS ME KATE
MAN IN THE DARK
DIAL M FOR MURDER
THE DIAMOND
MISS SADIE THOMPSON

And in more recent times…
THE STEWARDESSES
FLESH FOR FRANKENSTEIN
THE LOLLIPOP GIRLS IN HARD CANDY
THE PORNO HOSTESS IN 3-D
PARASITE
COMIN' AT YA

TEN VERY LONG AND QUITE RIDICULOUS FILM TITLES

1 **YOU'VE GOT TO WALK IT IF YOU LIKE TO TALK IT OR YOU'LL LOSE THAT BEAR** (1971)

2 **OH DAD, POOR DAD, MAMA'S HUNG YOU IN THE CLOSET AND I'M FEELING SO SAD** (1967)

3 **WILL HIERONYMOUS MERKIN EVER FORGET MERCY HUMPE AND FIND TRUE HAPPINESS?** (1969)

4 **I COULD NEVER HAVE SEX WITH ANY MAN WHO HAS SO LITTLE REGARD FOR MY HUSBAND** (1973)

5 **THE FILM THAT RISES TO THE SURFACE OF CLARIFIED BUTTER** (1968)

6 **BETTA, BETTA IN THE WALL, WHO'S THE FATTEST FISH OF ALL?** (1969)

7 **THE END OF THE WORLD IN OUR USUAL BED IN A NIGHT FULL OF RAIN** (1978)

8 **THE HEART OF A LADY AS PURE AS A FULL MOON OVER THE PLACE OF MEDICAL SALVATION** (A Far Eastern retitling of *'Not as a Stranger'*) (1955)

9 **THOSE MAGNIFICENT MEN IN THEIR FLYING MACHINES, OR HOW I FLEW FROM LONDON TO PARIS IN 25 HOURS AND 11 MINUTES** (1965)

10 **THE PERSECUTION AND ASSASSINATION OF JEAN-PAUL MARAT AS PERFORMED BY THE INMATES OF THE ASYLUM OF CHARENTON UNDER THE DIRECTION OF THE MARQUIS DE SADE** (1966)

Those Magnificent Men in Their Flying Machines

What more can we say? Possibly, readers may know of longer and/or even more ridiculous offerings, in which case the compilers would love to hear about them.

THE FAME IS IN THE NAME

Fifty performers who changed theirs to make it on the big screen.

If part of the job of being a movie performer is about creating and living an image, and if the sound and look of a name are essential ingredients of that image, then we can only say that it isn't too surprising that most of this lot opted for a name change. Julie Andrews would probably have made it all right as Julia Wells, ditto Barbara Stanwyck as Ruby Stevens and even Sterling Hayden as John Hamilton. It is difficult, however, to imagine Issur Damelovitch succeeding in a series of rugged he-man roles, or Bernard Schwartz as a dashing romantic lead. And what about Frederick Austerlitz and Virginia McMath as the world's best-loved dancing couple?

Screen Name (Real Name)
JUNE ALLYSON (Ella Geisman)
JULIE ANDREWS (Julia Wells)
FRED ASTAIRE (Frederick Austerlitz)
MARY ASTOR (Lucille V Langhanke)
CHARLES AZNAVOUR (Varenach Aznourian)
LAUREN BACALL (Betty Perske)
ANNE BANCROFT (Anna Maria Italiano)
CHARLES BRONSON (Charles Buchinsky)
GEORGE BURNS (Nathan Birnbaum)
ELLEN BURSTYN (Edna Rae Gillooly)
RED BUTTONS (Aaron Chwatt)
MICHAEL CAINE (Maurice Mickelwhite)
RORY CALHOUN (Francis Durgin)
DYAN CANNON (Samille Friesen)
CYD CHARISSE (Tula Finklea)
CLAUDETTE COLBERT (Lily Chauchoin)
TONY CURTIS (Bernard Schwartz)
DORIS DAY (Doris Kappelhoff)
SANDRA DEE (Alexandra Zuck)
BO DEREK (Mary Collins)
MARLENE DIETRICH (Maria Von Losch)
TROY DONAHUE (Merle Johnson)
KIRK DOUGLAS (Issur Damelovitch)
ALICE FAYE (Anne Leppert)
MITZI GAYNOR (Francesca Von Gerber)
CARY GRANT (Archibald Leach)
TY HARDIN (Orison Whipple Hungerford II)
STERLING HAYDEN (John Hamilton)
RITA HAYWORTH (Margarita Cansino)
ANNE HEYWOOD (Violet Pretty)
ROCK HUDSON (Ray Fitzgerald)

TAB HUNTER (Arthur Galien)
DANNY KAYE (David Kominski)
MICHAEL LANDON (Eugene Orowitz)
KARL MALDEN (Mladen Sekulovich)
DEAN MARTIN (Dino Crocetti)
WALTER MATTHAU (Walter Matuschanskayasky)
RAY MILLAND (Reginald Truscott-Jones)
HUGH O'BRIEN (Hugh Krampe)
JACK PALANCE (Walter Palannik)
SLIM PICKENS (Louis Bert Lindley Jr)
GINGER ROGERS (Virginia McMath)
MICKEY ROONEY (Joe Yule Jr)
JILL ST JOHN (Jill Oppenheim)
OMAR SHARIF (Michel Shalboub)
BARBARA STANWYCK (Ruby Stevens)
CONNIE STEVENS (Concetta Ingolia)
STELLA STEVENS (Estelle Eggleston)
GENE WILDER (Jerome Silberman)
NATALIE WOOD (Natasha Gurdin)

10 ENDURING MOVIE MONSTERS

DRACULA

The Vampire created in Bram Stoker's novel of the same title has been a staple character in the Cinema since 1921, when Max Schreck portrayed him in the German film 'Nosferatu'. Bela Lugosi made the role his own in the USA during the 1930s, and Christopher Lee also took out a long lease on it in his Hammer film appearances from 1958 to the early 70s. Dozens of other actors have donned the fangs for one or more appearances, including John Carradine, Lon Chaney Jr, Dennis Price, Jack Palance and David Niven. Recent notable portrayals have been by George Hamilton in 'Love at First Bite', Klaus Kinski in 'Nosferatu', and Frank Langella in a 1979 remake of the original story.

FRANKENSTEIN

Or more correctly, Frankenstein's Creature — Frankenstein being the scientist who actually put him together from bits and pieces of corpses. Boris Karloff established the visual image of the creature in 'Frankenstein' in 1931, and imitations have abounded in films from all over the world for the subsequent 50 years. Lon Chaney and Bela Lugosi also made appearances in the role, while Hammer's British versions of the creature included both Christopher Lee and Dave Prowse (who later became Darth Vader in 'Star Wars').

Christopher Lee

KING KONG

The giant with a host of human qualities — including tender loving care for Fay Wray and an understandably bad tempered contempt for the hordes of tiny humans who keep harrassing him — was the star of what is widely regarded as the all-time best monster movie, back in 1932. His legend was revived by the Japanese in the 1960s for 'King Kong Escapes' and 'King Kong Versus Godzilla' (excuses for lots of stomping destruction of tiny intricate modelwork), in which the King is pitted against, respectively, a robot replica of himself and a radioactive dinosaur, both of appropriately towering proportions. He saw them both off, of course. The original story was finally remade with much more technical expertise but notably less charisma in 1976, with Jessica Lange in the Fay Wray role as chief screamer.

With these three heavyweights out of the way, most of the other notable monsters of the movies are comparative also-rans, mostly making their presence felt in just one film, or else — like the fairly oft-seen werewolf — appearing to depict different representatives of a species rather than a consistently similar character. The following are the seven most notable of the runners-up to the 'big three':

THE BEAST FROM 20,000 FATHOMS

One of the originators of the American monster cycle of the 1950s, this beast was a rhedosaurus, an amphibious dinosaur who came out of Arctic deep freeze in the 1953 film named after him. Animated by Ray Harryhausen.

GODZILLA

A Japanese distant relative of The Beast, though a lot taller and equipped with fiery radioactive breath for spectacular effects. He has already been mentioned as a one time adversary of King Kong, and in fact stomped on various districts of Tokyo through quite a few films.

GORGO

Another relative of the above two, this one bears mentioning because it (or *she*, as the plot makes clear) is a British dinosaur, in the eponymous film of 1960. A small version, Gorgo Jr, is caught by fishermen and displayed in a London carnival: the cue for mum to appear, taking Tower Bridge and much of London literally in her stride as she comes to collect baby.

THE WEREWOLF

As mentioned above, never a consistent character. There have been a variety of different werewolves and wolfmen in films, usually ordinary bods who undergo rapid hair-and-fang growth and develop an unfortunate bloodlust whenever the moon shines full. Notable film interpretations have included 'The Wolf Man' in 1941 with Lon Chaney Jr; the famous teenage exploitation flick 'I Was a Teenage Werewolf' in 1957; Oliver Reed in Hammer's 'Curse of the Werewolf' in 1961; and the recent 'An American Werewolf in London', the absolutely staggering transformation scenes of which justifiably won it an Oscar for special effects make-up

THE THING FROM ANOTHER WORLD

The star of Howard Hawks' famous 1951 production was a space-travelling humanoid vegetable, looming some 6½ feet tall because he was really James Arness. A bunch of US Air Force incompetents actually had little trouble in electrocuting him out of circulation, but he remains memorable because the film evoked splendidly the shiver-down-the-back atmosphere of a small group stuck miles from anywhere (the Arctic) in constant fear of finding the errant and irritable Mr Veg lurking behind the next door they open. The film was played for tingles rather than horror, which is probably why it is still remembered better than its host of imitators.

THE GIANT CLAW

This claw (the title of the film) belongs to an equally giant extraterrestrial bird, fondly remembered because (a) the film's plot and direction seemed to be the work of a three year-old, (b) the said bird had bulbous, staring eyes which instantly reminded everybody who saw later TV re-runs, of Marty Feldman, and (c) as an all-powerful monstrosity, the thing was hopelessly inept. At the climax of the film, despite having travelled to Earth at the speed of light, the bird fails to overtake and destroy the Dakota aircraft firing the special anti-matter gun which eventually kills it. The all-time incompetent monster.

THE MUMMY

Again appearing in several variations through the years — though always emerging from a desecrated Egyptian tomb to throttle most of the desecrators — the Mummy is another enduring monster figure of the movies. Boris Karloff took the first bandage-swathed role in 'The Mummy' in 1932, Lon Chaney Jr reprised it three times in the 40s, and Christopher Lee donned the plaster-castings for Hammer's late 50s British remake.

THE FILMS OF RONALD REAGAN

Ronald Reagan is currently enjoying his most successful starring role ever, but he has a long list of less memorable appearances for the public to look back upon. Most of the films below are workmanlike Hollywood B-features, dividing broadly into romantic adventures, war stories and Westerns. Reagan's performances in 'King's Row' and 'The Hasty Heart' have been pinpointed as his most sensitive, but unlike many of his Hollywood contemporaries, he never actually got the chance to *play* the President of the United States.

? ? ? ? ? ? ? ?

LOVE IS ON THE AIR (1937)
SUBMARINE D-1 (1937)
SERGEANT MURPHY (1938)
SWING YOUR LADY (1938)
HOLLYWOOD HOTEL (1938)

ACCIDENTS WILL HAPPEN (1938)
COWBOY FROM BROOKLYN (1938)
BOY MEETS GIRL (1938)
GIRLS ON PROBATION (1938)
BROTHER RAT (1938)
GOING PLACES (1938)
SECRET SERVICE OF THE AIR (1939)
DARK VICTORY (1939)
CODE OF THE SECRET SERVICE (1939)
NAUGHTY BUT NICE (1939)
HELL'S KITCHEN (1939)
ANGELS WASH THEIR FACES (1939)
SMASHING THE MONEY RING (1939)
BROTHER RAT AND A BABY (1940)
AN ANGEL FROM TEXAS (1940)
MURDER IN THE AIR (1940)
KNUTE ROCKNE (1940)
TUGBOAT ANNIE SAILS AGAIN (1940)
SANTA FE TRAIL (1940)
THE BAD MAN (1941)
MILLION DOLLAR BABY (1941)
NINE LIVES ARE NOT ENOUGH (1941)
INTERNATIONAL SQUADRON (1941)
KING'S ROW (1942)
JUKE GIRL (1942)
DESPERATE JOURNEY (1942)
THIS IS THE ARMY (1943)
STALLION ROAD(1947)
THAT HAGEN GIRL (1947)
THE VOICE OF THE TURTLE (1947)
JOHN LOVES MARY (1949)
NIGHT UNTO NIGHT (1949)
THE GIRL FROM JONES BEACH (1949)
IT'S A GREAT FEELING (1949)
THE HASTY HEART (1950)
LOUISA (1950)
STORM WARNING (1951)
BEDTIME FOR BONZO (1951)
THE LAST OUTPOST (1951)
HONG KONG (1952)
THE WINNING TEAM (1952)
SHE'S WORKING HER WAY THROUGH COLLEGE (1952)
TROPIC ZONE (1953)
LAW AND ORDER (1953)
PRISONER OF WAR (1954)
CATTLE QUEEN OF MONTANA (1954)
TENNESSEE'S PARTNER (1955)
HELLCATS OF THE NAVY (1957)
THE KILLERS (1964)

THE MAGNIFICENT SEVEN

1. **YUL BRYNNER**
2. **ROBERT VAUGHN**
3. **CHARLES BRONSON**
4. **HORST BUCHHOLZ**
5. **STEVE McQUEEN**
6. **JAMES COBURN**
7. **BRAD DEXTER**

Yul Brunner and Horst Buchholz

'The Magnificent Seven' was a translation into the American Western idiom of Akira Kurosawa's 1954 Japanese classic 'The Seven Samurai' — a fable of mediaeval Japan which told of seven mighty knights facing hordes of enemies in the defence of an innocent village.

The 1961 Western simply turned the Samurai into gunfighters — played by the actors above — and the locale into a terrorised Mexican border village, before retelling the story. Although Yul Brynner was the only really big star name among them at this time, most of the others were destined for top box office success during the next decade — notably Bronson, Coburn and Steve McQueen, who at the time of his death in 1981 was one of the three highest paid actors in the world.

THE HOLLYWOOD TEN

In 1947, during the McCarthy era in America, people from all walks of life were called before the Un-American Activities Committee to provide reassurance and proof that they were not Communists. This Committee of the House of Representatives subpoenaed Charlie Chaplin, for instance, who sent back the somewhat incensed reply, 'I have never joined any political party or organization in my life. I am what you call a peace-monger.' The result was that Chaplin's re-entry visa was withdrawn when he eventually left the country to film 'Limelight' in Britain.

In Hollywood, a group of directors, writers and producers collectively followed the same line as Chaplin and, invoking the 5th Amendment, refused to testify about their political convictions. The repercussions included short prison sentences, followed by virtual ostracism in Hollywood, since it was felt to be politically indelicate to give them work. The ten in question are listed below.

ALVAH BESSIE	**HOWARD LAWSON**
HERBERT BIBERMAN	**ALBERT MALTZ**
LESTER COLE	**SAM ORNITZ**
EDWARD DMYTRYK	**ADRIAN SCOTT**
RING LARDNER JR.	**DALTON TRUMBO**

173

THE DIRTY DOZEN

1 **JOHN CASSAVETES** (VICTOR FRANKO)
2 **CHARLES BRONSON** (JOSEPH WLADISLAW)
3 **JIM BROWN** (ROBERT JEFFERSON)
4 **TELLY SAVALAS** (ARCHER MAGGOTT)
5 **DONALD SUTHERLAND** (VERNON PINKLEY)
6 **CLINT WALKER** (SAMSON POSEY)
7 **TRINI LOPEZ** (PEDRO JIMINEZ)
8 **TOM BUSBY** (MILO VLADEK)
9 **BENITO CARRUTHERS** (GLENN GILPIN)
10 **STUART COOPER** (ROSCOE LEVER)
11 **COLIN MAITLAND** (SETH SAWYER)
12 **AL MANCINI** (TASSOS BRAVOS)

The biggest American box office success in 1967, 'The Dirty Dozen' was a Second World War theme notable both for its brutality (the main characters were dangerous convicted criminals, released specifically to cause maximum death and destruction on a near-suicidal mission) and for the number of big-name players who were persuaded to portray the crooked comrades-in-arms. Most of them (the characters, not the actors) predictably came to grief during the course of the film.

The name in brackets beside each actor is that of the character he played in the film.

Clint Walker and Lee Marvin

THE BOWERY BOYS

1	LEO GORCEY	6	DAVID GORCEY
2	HUNTZ HALL	7	BOBBY JORDAN
3	BILLY BENEDICT	8	STANLEY CLEMENTS
4	GABRIEL DELL	9	BENNIE BARTLETT
5	BERNARD GORCEY		

Developing out of an earlier aggregation called the Dead End Kids, who made their debut in the 1937 film 'Dead End' supporting Humphrey Bogart, the Bowery Boys (named after the poor New York district where their adventures took place) were a set of comic semi-delinquents who starred in almost 50 rapidly-made films in the immediate post-war period.

Huntz Hall was the acknowledged leader of the troupe, and their billing became 'Huntz Hall and The Bowery Boys' at some stage along the way. In later years their antics would certainly have graced a TV series rather than the cinema screen, and in fact the low budget Bowery movies were early sales to TV on both sides of the Atlantic during the 1950s.

SOME OF 'OUR GANG'

ALFALFA SWITZER
STYMIE BEARD
SCOTTY BECKETT
JACKIE COOPER
JACKIE CONDON
WHEEZER COBB
TOUGHIE DAVIS
JOHNNY DOWNS
MICKEY DANIELS
DARLA HOOD
PORKY LEE
MICKEY GUBITOSI
MARY KORNMAN
SUNSHINE SAMMY MORRISON
BUCKWHEAT THOMAS
PINEAPPLE JACKSON
FARINA HOPKINS
WALDO SMITH
WALLY ALBRIGHT JR.
MICKEY ROONEY

'Our Gang' was a group of child actors put together during the 1920s by producer Hal Roach for a series of silent slapstick comedy shorts. The team was constantly changing, though as a concept they remained in vogue (and in work) through the 1930s and into the 40s. Many 'Our Gang' graduates went on to successful solo work in the cinema, with Mickey Rooney and Mickey Gubitosi (who, on reaching adulthood, changed his name to Robert Blake and subsequently starred in the TV series 'Baretta' and films like 'In Cold Blood' and 'Tell Them Willie Boy Is Here') standing out as the biggest star names to have emerged from the ranks.

SOME INTRIGUING CHANGES OF TITLE

(1)   American film titles changed for the British market

HOUSE OF HORRORS to **JOAN MEDFORD IS MISSING**
CRY UNCLE to **SUPER DICK**
CHICAGO MASQUERADE to **LITTLE EGYPT**
PARDON US to **JAILBIRDS**
NEVER GIVE A SUCKER AN EVEN BREAK to **WHAT A MAN**
MR WRINKLE GOES TO WAR to **ARMS AND THE WOMAN**
THUNDER IN THE VALLEY to **BOB, SON OF BATTLE**
SWING SHIFT MAISIE to **THE GIRL IN OVERALLS**
THE STRIPPER to **WOMAN OF SUMMER**
THE WAC FROM WALLA WALLA to **ARMY CAPERS**
SMASH-UP to **A WOMAN DESTROYED**
OFF LIMITS to **MILITARY POLICEMAN**
THE COCKEYED MIRACLE to **MR GRIGGS RETURNS**
AN AMERICAN GUERILLA IN THE PHILLIPINES to **I SHALL RETURN**
ARTISTS AND MODELS ABROAD to **STRANDED IN PARIS**
A GIRL, A GUY AND A GOB to **THE NAVY STEPS OUT**
I DOOD IT to **BY HOOK OR BY CROOK**
I MARRIED A COMMUNIST to **THE WOMAN ON PIER 13**
THE POPPY IS ALSO A FLOWER to **DANGER GROWS WILD**
SOUTHWEST PASSAGE to **CAMELS WEST**

In some cases these have so little to connect them, that it almost seems that the new titles must have been drawn out of a hat. Some of the changes were probably made for the simple reason that the originals were so incomprehensible that audiences might have howled with laughter at the title instead of going to see the film. For further evidence, here are some examples of changes in the opposite direction.

(2)   British film titles changed for the American market

BEAT GIRL to **WILD FOR KICKS**
DARK EYES OF LONDON to **THE HUMAN MONSTER**
ON THE FIDDLE to **OPERATION SNAFU**
FANNY BY GASLIGHT to **MAN OF EVIL**
JUMP FOR GLORY to **WHEN THIEF MEETS THIEF**
I LIVE IN GROSVENOR SQUARE to **A YANK IN LONDON**
ROCKETS GALORE to **MAD LITTLE ISLAND**
MY DAUGHTER JOY to **IF THIS BE SIN**
A MATTER OF LIFE AND DEATH to **STAIRWAY TO HEAVEN**
A TERRIBLE BEAUTY to **NIGHT FIGHTERS**
THE SMALLEST SHOW ON EARTH to **BIG TIME OPERATORS**
THE WHITE UNICORN to **BAD SISTER**
TWINKY to **LOLA**
HOME AT SEVEN to **MURDER ON MONDAY**
GRAND NATIONAL NIGHT to **WICKED WIFE**

COSH BOY to **THE SLASHER**
NIGHT OF THE EAGLE to **BURN WITCH, BURN**
THE IRON MAIDEN to **THE SWINGIN' MAIDEN**
KNAVE OF HEARTS to **LOVER BOY**
TEHERAN to **THE PLOT TO KILL ROOSEVELT**

Again, few of these seem on the surface to display much logic except for an apparent American penchant for comic-book directness in place of any hint of subtlety. Finally, just to make us all wonder why they really bothered....

(3)   Some changes which were hardly worth the trouble
TWENTY ONE DAYS to **TWENTY ONE DAYS TOGETHER**
THE VICIOUS CIRCLE to **THE CIRCLE**
STRANGE INTERLUDE to **STRANGE INTERVAL**
THE FORSYTE SAGA to **THAT FORSYTE WOMAN**
WHITE SAVAGE to **WHITE CAPTIVE**
THE BACHELOR DAUGHTERS to **BACHELOR GIRLS**
BLUE DENIM to **BLUE JEANS**
DEADLINE USA to **DEADLINE**
THE CLOCK to **UNDER THE CLOCK**
DINO to **KILLER DINO**

REPEATED SUCCESSES

THE JAMES BOND FILMS

With the exception of 'Casino Royale', these films represent a continuous series of productions from the same source, being produced by the Harry Saltzman/Albert Broccoli partnership (Broccoli alone on the most recent ones) for United Artists. Over 20 years, it has proved to be one of the most rewarding film series ever in financial terms, and as regards box office popularity.

Virtually all the series of Bond books written by the creator of the character, Ian Fleming, have now been used up (although one short piece, 'Octopussy', is still a probable candidate), and it remains to be seen whether the producers will eventually lay the series to rest (unlikely), move on to Bond stories originating from other authors (including Kingsley Amis), or else turn to original scripts laid within the Fleming idiom. Since the actual storylines of the films have diverged from Fleming's originals ever more widely over the years — eventually having little but title and basic idea in common with them — the latter course seems the most likely.

'Casino Royale' is an oddity because as the first Bond book written, in the early 50s, it had its film rights sold far in advance of the other works, although the option on these rights was not taken up for many years. When the Bond series proper was launched to huge success, 'Casino Royale' was dusted off and filmed to cash in on the boom. It bore little relation to standard Bond films, and even less to Fleming's book, being a pure hokum-filled spoof on the whole genre of glamorous, gadgetty espionage films launched by Bond, and at its height in the mid-swingin' 60s.

The character of Bond was played by Sean Connery in the first four films, and in 'You Only Live Twice' and 'Diamonds Are Forever'. Little-known actor George Lazenby was tried out (none too successfully) in 'On Her Majesty's Secret Service', while Roger Moore has taken the role in all the films from 'Live and Let Die' onwards. The role of Bond in 'Casino Royale' is hard to pinpoint, since virtually every character in the film is called 'James Bond' — but David Niven, playing an older JB in retirement, seems to be the closest the film gets towards identifying its ostensible lead character.

DR NO (1962)
FROM RUSSIA WITH LOVE (1963)
GOLDFINGER (1964)
THUNDERBALL (1965)
CASINO ROYALE (1967)
YOU ONLY LIVE TWICE (1967)
ON HER MAJESTY'S SECRET SERVICE (1970)
DIAMONDS ARE FOREVER (1971)
LIVE AND LET DIE (1973)
THE MAN WITH THE GOLDEN GUN (1974)
THE SPY WHO LOVED ME (1977)
MOONRAKER (1979)
FOR YOUR EYES ONLY (1981)

Sean Connery

PERFORMERS WHO BEGAN AS CHILD STARS

"Doc" Bishop and
Shirley Temple

MARY PICKFORD (in *'Her First Biscuits'* at age 15)
JACKIE COOGAN (in *'The Kid'* at age 6)
SHIRLEY TEMPLE (in *'The Red-haired Alibi'* at age 3)
JACKIE COOPER (in the *'Our Gang'* films at age 6)
MICKEY ROONEY (in short films as *'Mickey McGuire'* at age 6)
JANE WITHERS (in *'Bright Eyes'* at age 7)
JUDY GARLAND (in *'Every Sunday'* at age 13)
RODDY McDOWALL (in *'Murder in the Family'* at age 8)
DONALD O'CONNOR (in *'Sing You Sinners'* at age 12)
NATALIE WOOD (in *'Happy Land'* at age 5)
HAYLEY MILLS (in *'Tiger Bay'* at age 12)
MARK LESTER (in *'Allez France'* at age 6)
JACK WILD (in *'Oliver!'* at age 14)
TATUM O'NEAL (in *'Paper Moon'* at age 10)
FREDDIE BARTHOLOMEW (in *'Fascination'* at age 6)
ELIZABETH TAYLOR (in *'There's One Born Every Minute'* at age 10)
MANDY MILLER (in *'The Man in the White Suit'* at age 7)
GERALDINE CHAPLIN (in *'Limelight'* at age 8)
PAMELA FRANKLIN (in *'The Innocents'* at age 12)
JAMES FOX (in *'The Magnet'* as William Fox at age 10)

Most of these performers went on to adult careers in the movies, though for some
— and Shirley Temple is the obvious example — it was their juvenile period
which provided the basis of their enduring fame. There have been many other
children in films through the years, of course, including hundreds who made just
one appearance in a single film, but the list above covers most of those who made
a noticeable contribution to the cinema.

The under-age trend is by no means dead, though no longer as common an
occurrence as it used to be, and there are pint-sized performers on the screen
today who look like following those on the list and continuing their screen career
into adulthood. The most notable example is probably Ricky Schroeder, who
made a strong impact in 'The Champ' and remains a hot Hollywood property.

DIRECTORS WHO HAVE APPEARED IN THEIR OWN FILMS

(Not including actors who have gone on to direct, or directors like Chaplin who were acknowledged performers as well.)

ALFRED HITCHCOCK (fleeting cameos in more than 60% of his films)
TONY RICHARDSON (in 'Tom Jones')
ROBERT ALDRICH (in 'The Big Knife')
CECIL B De MILLE (in 'Variety Girl', 'Son of Paleface' and 'Sunset Boulevard')
JOHN HUSTON (in 'The Bible' and 'The Treasure of the Sierra Madre')
FRANK BORZAGE (in 'Jeanne Eagels')
INGMAR BERGMAN (in 'Waiting Women')
JEAN RENOIR (in 'La Regle du Jeu')
PRESTON STURGES (in 'Paris Holiday' and 'Sullivan's Travels')
ROMAN POLANSKI (in 'The Tenant')

Even if most directors possess a large helping of megalomania as a requisite of being successful at their job, their ego generally deflates when they are placed in front of a camera lens. Although the list above is not exhaustive, the number of directors who have appeared on screen in their own films is fairly small. Most of the above only showed themselves in a single film, and some of those appearances were fleeting. Hitchcock is quite definitely the exception to the rule, as he was to so many others. 'Hitch-spotting' has become quite a familiar pastime during showings of his films, so varied and ingenious were the ways in which his cameo was inserted within the action.

Hitchcock and Hitchcock

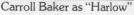

STARS WHO HAVE HAD FILMS MADE OF THEIR LIFE STORIES

Hollywood coined the term 'biopic' (from 'biographical picture', naturally enough) to describe a film which told a true life story in dramatic terms (as opposed to a straight documentary). Biopics have of course been made about virtually every great figure in history, but with the film industry itself now well on the way to its first century, several of the medium's own stellar fraternity have also come in for the treatment.

Historical accuracy is usually claimed in general rather than in detail for such productions; dramatic licence can be a convenient excuse to cover a multitude of sins (or uncover them, in some cases). It has to be said that, in general, biopics through the years have come in for critical hammering, and many in fact were probably doomed from the start. After all, how many peoples' lives, even those of Hollywood stars, have the consistent pattern of a well-balanced story?

Carroll Baker as "Harlow"

Marilyn Monroe

HUMPHREY BOGART — *'Bogie'*, with Kevin O'Connor as Bogart (1980)
JEAN HARLOW — *'Harlow'*, with Carroll Baker as Harlow (1965)
W.C. FIELDS — *'W.C. Fields and Me'*, with Rod Steiger as Fields (1976)
MARILYN MONROE — *'Goodbye Norma Jean'*, with Misty Rowe as Monroe (1975)

BUSTER KEATON — *'The Buster Keaton Story'*, with Donald O'Connor as Keaton (1957)

CLARK CABLE and **CAROLE LOMBARD** — *'Gable and Lombard'*, withJames Brolin as Gable and Jill Clayburgh as Lombard (1976)

AL JOLSON — *'The Jolson Story'*, with Larry Parks as Jolson (1946)

ELVIS PRESLEY — *'Elvis: The Movie'* with Kurt Russell as Presley (1978)

GEORGE RAFT — *'The George Raft Story'*, with Ray Danton as Raft (1961)

BRUCE LEE — *'The Bruce Lee Story'*, with Hsiao Lung as Lee (1974)

RUDOLPH VALENTINO — *'Valentino'*, with Rudolf Nureyev as Valentino (1977)

LON CHANEY — *'The Man of a Thousand Faces'*, with James Cagney as Chaney (1957)

WILL ROGERS — *'The Story of Will Rogers'*, with his son, Will Jr., as Rogers (1950)

ACTORS WHO HAVE PLAYED THEMSELVES IN FILMS

HUMPHREY BOGART in *'The Love Lottery'* (1954)
GRETA GARBO in *'A Man's Man'* (1929)
PAUL NEWMAN in *'Silent Movie'* (1976)
CARY GRANT in *'Without Reservations'* (1946)

John and Lionel Barrymore

GLORIA SWANSON in *'Hollywood'* (1923)
GARY COOPER in *'Variety Girl'* (1947)
ANNE BANCROFT in *'Silent Movie'* (1976)
ELLIOTT GOULD in *'Nashville'* (1975)
BRIGITTE BARDOT in *'Dear Brigitte'* (1965)
LIONEL BARRYMORE in *'Free and Easy'* (1930)
KATHARINE HEPBURN in *'Stage Door Canteen'* (1943)
TOMMY STEELE in *'Kill Me Tomorrow'* (1955)
JULIE CHRISTIE in *'Nashville'* (1975)
BEN TURPIN in *'Hollywood'* (1923)
NATALIE WOOD in *'The Candidate'* (1972)
BOB HOPE in *'The Oscar'* (1966)
SUSANNAH YORK in *'Long Shot'* (1978)
GENE KELLY in *'Love Is Better Than Ever'* (1952)
LIV ULLMANN in *'Players'* (1979)
JACKIE COOGAN in *'Free and Easy'* (1930)

The 20 examples listed above are but a small sample of the many instances from the 1920s to date when actors and actresses have played themselves, normally in cameo roles designed to lend fidelity to a fictional story. Certain films through the years have been designed expressly to show a host of well-known stars as themselves, notably 'Variety Girl', 'Silent Movie', 'Stage Door Canteen' (a semi-documentary), and several offerings with the word 'Hollywood' in the title. Some of the appearances in these films are listed above; lengths vary but they tend to be fairly fleeting, particularly when a large number are involved in the same movie.

NON-ACTORS WHO HAVE PLAYED DRAMATIC ROLES IN FILMS

MICKEY SPILLANE in *'The Girl Hunters'* (1963)
GRAHAM GREENE in *'Day for Night'* (1973)
JOMO KENYATTA in *'Sanders of the River'* (1935)
JEAN SHRIMPTON in *'Privilege'* (1967)
LEON TROTSKY in *'The Battle Cry of Peace'* (1915)
MARGARET TRUDEAU in *'The Guardian Angel'* (1978)
TRUMAN CAPOTE in *'Murder by Death'* (1976)
QUENTIN CRISP in *'Hamlet'* (1976)
XAVIERA HOLLANDER in *'My Pleasure Is My Business'* (1974)
GERMAINE GREER in *'Universal Soldier'* (1971)
JACQUELINE SUSANN in *'Valley of the Dolls'* (1967)

MAYOR JOHN LINDSAY in *'Rosebud'* (1975)
MANDY RICE-DAVIES in *'Kuni Lemel in Tel Aviv'* (1976)
DAVID FROST in *'The VIPs'* (1963)
PETER BENCHLEY in *'Jaws'* (1975)

The main difference between this list and the previous one is that all these personalities from outside the acting profession were used in fictional roles, rather than simply playing themselves. Many of the parts were small cameos (Peter Benchley, for example, played a reporter in a scene from the film of his own story 'Jaws'), but one or two of the examples above represent major acting roles. Mickey Spillane, for instance, played his own tough detective Mike Hammer — the film's leading part — in 'The Girl Hunters'.

NON-ACTING PERSONALITIES WHO HAVE PLAYED THEMSELVES IN FILMS

MUHAMMAD ALI in *'The Greatest'* (1977)
MICHAEL FOOT in *'Rockets Galore'* (1958)
HUGH HEFNER in *'How Did a Nice Girl Like You Ever Get Into This Business'* (1970)
JOHN FORD in *'Big Time'* (1929)
STIRLING MOSS in *'The Beauty Contest'* (1964)
ILIE NASTASE in *'Players'* (1979)
CARLOS REUTEMANN in *'Speed Fever'* (1978)
JIMMY YOUNG in *'Otley'* (1968)
JIM LOVELL (the Apollo astronaut) in *'The Man Who Fell to Earth'* (1976)
BERNARD LEVIN in *'Nothing But the Best'* (1963)
GILBERT HARDING in *'Expresso Bongo'* (1959)
JOE FRAZIER in *'Rocky'* (1977)
BILLY GRAHAM in *'Two a Penny'* (1967)
HEDDA HOPPER in *'Sunset Boulevard'* (1950)
AMY JOHNSON in *'Dual Control'* (1932)
HELEN KELLER in *'Deliverance'* (1919)
ARNOLD PALMER in *'Call Me Bwana'* (1963)
GODFREY WINN in *'Billy Liar'* (1963)

JOAN BAKEWELL in *'The Touchables'* (1967)
LORD BADEN-POWELL in *'The Man Who Changed His Mind'* (1928)

The above 20 are only a selection from scores of people outside the acting profession who have been asked at some time to appear as themselves in films. The idea was going strong in the pre-First World War silents, and shows no signs of dying out today. Generally, these guest celebrities were not asked to do anything out of character, but simply to 'act naturally'. There is much filmed evidence that this simple instruction is all that many people need to turn on a totally embarrassing artificialilty, or do their darnedest to out-ham the professionals they are pitted against.

10 MEMORABLE ONE-LINERS

1 **'FRANKLY, MY DEAR, I DON'T GIVE A DAMN!'**
(Clark Gable as Rhett Butler to Vivien Leigh as Scarlett O'Hara in *'Gone With the Wind'*)
2 **'IF YOU WANT ANYTHING JUST WHISTLE. YOU KNOW HOW TO WHISTLE DON'T YOU? YOU JUST PUT YOUR LIPS TOGETHER AND BLOW.'**
(Lauren Bacall to Humphrey Bogart in *'To Have and Have Not'*)
3 **'I'LL MAKE HIM AN OFFER HE CAN'T REFUSE.'**
(Marlon Brando to Robert Duvall in *'The Godfather'*)
4 **'LOVE MEANS NEVER HAVING TO SAY YOU'RE SORRY'**
(Ali MacGraw to Ryan O'Neal in *'Love Story'*)
5 **'SO ELAINE ROBINSON GOT STARTED IN A FORD'**
(Dustin Hoffman to Anne Bancroft in *'The Graduate'*)
6 **'MAY THE FORCE BE WITH YOU'**
(Alec Guinness to Mark Hamill in *'Star Wars'*)
7 **'IS THAT A GUN IN YOUR POCKET OR ARE YOU JUST GLAD TO SEE ME?'**
(Mae West in *'She Done Him Wrong'*)
8 **'WOULD YOU LIKE A LEG OR A BREAST?'**
(Grace Kelly to Cary Grant in *'To Catch a Thief'* — she was talking about the food)
9 **'HOW ABOUT "WELCOME TO CALIFORNIA"?'**
(Jack Kruschen, debating what to say to the Martians in *'War of the Worlds'*)
10 **'SHE CUT OFF HER NIPPLES WITH GARDEN SHEARS — YOU CALL THAT NORMAL?'**
(Elizabeth Taylor to Marlon Brando in *'Reflections in a Golden Eye'*)

Gable's final line in 'Gone With the Wind' introduced profanity to the cinema; so much so that the film was condemned by the Catholic Legion of Decency, making it a mortal sin for Catholics to see it.

10 MEMORABLE OFF SCREEN QUOTES BY ACTORS

1 **RICHARD BURTON:** "Certainly most movie executives were making love to starlets — but then, so were most of us actors."
2 **RUDOLPH VALENTINO:** "A man should control his life: mine is controlling me!"
3 **MICKEY ROONEY:** "I was a fourteen year-old boy for thirty years."
4 **HUMPHREY BOGART:** "I don't trust any bastard who doesn't drink."
5 **WARREN BEATTY:** "Movies are fun, but they're not a cure for cancer."
6 **CHARLIE CHAPLIN:** "I have no further use for America; I wouldn't go back there if Jesus Christ was President."
7 **JOHN BARRYMORE:** "There are lots of methods. Mine involves a lot of talent, a glass, and some cracked ice."
8 **LIONEL BARRYMORE:** "Well, I've played everything but a harp."
9 **BERT LAHR:** "After 'The Wizard of Oz' I was typecast as a lion, and there aren't all that many parts for lions."
10 **PETER COOK:** "I don't like watching rape and violence in the cinema. I get enough of them at home."

10 MEMORABLE OFF SCREEN QUOTES BY ACTRESSES

1 **SOPHIA LOREN:** "Sex appeal is 50% what you've got, and 50% what people think you've got."
2 **KATHARINE HEPBURN:** "Show me an actress who isn't a personality, and I'll show you a woman who isn't a star."
3 **ELIZABETH TAYLOR:** "I don't pretend to be an ordinary housewife."
4 **MARILYN MONROE:** "To put it bluntly, I seem to be a whole superstructure with no foundation — but I'm working on the foundation."
5 **JANE FONDA:** "You spend all your life trying to do something they put people in asylums for."
6 **SHIRLEY MacLAINE** (on the Academy Awards): "Oh, the voting is legitimate, but there's the sentimentality. One year when Elizabeth Taylor got a hole in her throat, I cancelled my plane reservations."
7 **HEDY LAMARR:** "Any girl can look glamorous. All she has to do is stand still and look stupid."
8 **TALLULAH BANKHEAD:** "I'm as pure as the driven slush."
9 **MARGARET O'BRIEN:** "When I cry, do you want the tears to run all the way, or shall I stop halfway down?"
10 **CANDICE BERGEN:** "I may not be a great actress, but I've become the greatest at screen orgasms. Ten seconds of heavy breathing, roll your head from side to side, simulate a slight asthma attack, and die a little."

Jane Fonda

Michael Winner

10 MEMORABLE QUOTES BY DIRECTORS AND PRODUCERS

1 **MICHAEL WINNER:** "A team effort is a lot of people doing what I say."
2 **ALFRED HITCHCOCK:** "Actors? Cattle."
3 **D.W. GRIFFITH:** "There is no suspense like the suspense of delayed coition."
4 **HOWARD HUGHES** (about Jane Russell): "There are two good reasons why men will go to see her."
5 **CECIL B. De MILLE:** "Give me a couple of pages of the Bible and I'll give you a picture."
6 **HARRY COHN:** "I don't have ulcers — I give them!"
7 **DAVID O. SELZNICK:** "I have never gone after honours instead of dollars — but I have understood the relationship between them."
8 **DARRYL F. ZANUCK** "Don't say yes until I've finished talking"
9 **MICHAEL WINNER:** "If you want art, don't mess around with movies. Buy a Picasso."
10 **DAVID O. SELZNICK:** "It's rather symbolic of Hollywood that Tara was just a facade, with no rooms inside."

MEMORABLE QUOTES ATTRIBUTED TO SAM GOLDWYN

"A verbal contract isn't worth the paper it's written on."
"I can answer you in two words — im possible."
"Gentlemen — include me out."
"Let's bring it up-to-date with some snappy 19th Century dialogue."
"What we want is a story that starts with an earthquake and works its way up to a climax."
"Tell me, how did you love the picture?"
"Never let that bastard in here — unless we need him!"
"We've all passed a lot of water since then."

Goldwyn, Lasky, Zukor and Colleagues

MUCH PLAYED PARTS

SHERLOCK HOLMES

(Date of first appearance in the role is shown in brackets.)

MAURICE COSTELLO (1903)
GEORGES TREVILLE (1912)
HARRY BENHAM (1913)
JAMES BRAGINGTON (1914)
FRANCIS FORD (1914)
WILLIAM GILLETTE (1916)
H.A. SAINTSBURY (1916)
SAM ROBINSON (1918)

EILLE NORWOOD (1921)
JOHN BARRYMORE (1922)
CLIVE BROOK (1929)
CARLYLE BLACKWELL (1929)
ARTHUR WONTNER (1931)
RAYMOND MASSEY (1931)
ROBERT RENDEL (1932)
RICHARD GORDON (1933)

REGINALD OWEN (1933)
BASIL RATHBONE (1939)
JOHN LONGDEN (1951)
PETER CUSHING (1959)
CHRISTOPHER LEE (1962)
JEROME RAPHEL (1965)
JOHN NEVILLE (1965)
ROBERT STEPHENS (1970)
GEORGE C. SCOTT (1972)
STEWART GRANGER (1972)

KEITH McCONNELL (1974)
HARRY REEMS (1975)
DOUGLAS WILMER (1975)
ROGER MOORE (1976)
NICOL WILLIAMSON (1977)
TREVOR AINSLEY (1978)
PETER COOK (1978)
CHRISTOPHER PLUMMER (1979)
JEREMY YOUNG (1979)

This listing ignores portrayals of Holmes in foreign language films by non English speaking actors; were these included, its length would probably double. Countries like Denmark, France, Germany, Italy, even Czechoslovakia and Russia have all made Holmes films; in fact, in the early (pre-1920) days of the cinema, foreign productions far outnumbered American or British ones.

The most prolific Holmes portrayers were Eille Norwood and Basil Rathbone, with 47 and 14 films in the role respectively; Norwood's were mainly short features adhering closely to Conan Doyle's original stories, all made in Britain and all silent. Rathbone remains Hollywood's definitive version of the detective.

Peter Cushing only played Holmes once on the large screen, in Hammer's version of 'The Hound of the Baskervilles', though he later became familiar on British TV in the role. Much less characteristic portrayals were by black actor Sam Robinson (appropriately, in 'Black Sherlock Holmes'), and by Harry Reems in a porno version! Finally, the only actor to have portrayed both Holmes and Watson (in different films, obviously, though in successive years), was Reginald Owen.

Basil Rathbone

Johnny Weissmuller and
Maureen O'Sullivan

TARZAN

Edgar Rice Burroughs' jungle adventure remains one of the most popular creations of 20th Century literature, so it is not surprising that the is probably also the cinema's most-played heroic character, from Elmo Lincoln's silent opener in 1918, through the Olympian feats of the prodigious Johnny Weissmuller, to the modern sexual athlete portrayed by Miles O'Keefe opposite Bo Derek in 'Tarzan the Ape Man', 1981's version of the tale.

The number of Tarzan films so far made runs to almost three figures, and while the dates shown below indicate each actor's first appearance in the role, several of them repeated it through a whole series of films, the best-remembered being the most prolific — Johnny Weissmuller (12 times), Lex Barker (5) and Gordon Scott (5). Ron Ely became widely know as TV's Tarzan during the 1960s, and his two 1970 feature films in the role were adaptations of the TV series.

ELMO LINCOLN (1918)	**AZAD** (1959)
GENE POLLAR (1920)	**JOCK MAHONEY** (1962)
P. DEMPSEY TABLER (1920)	**RUDOLPH HRUSINSKY** (1962)
JAMES PIERCE (1927)	**INDRAJEET** (1963)
FRANK MERRILL (1928)	**KIT MORRIS** (1963)
CHARLIE CHASE (1932)	**JOE ROBINSON** (1963)
JOHNNY WEISSMULLER (1932)	**VLADIMIR KORENEV** (1963)
BUSTER CRABBE (1933)	**BRICK BARDO** (1964)
HERMAN BRIX (1934)	**DON BRAGG** (1964)
JOHN CAVAS (1937)	**TAYLOR MEAD** (1964)
GLENN MORRIS (1938)	**DARA SINGH** (1965)
MANEK (1938)	**RALPH HUDSON** (1965)
PENG FEI (1940)	**MIKE HENRY** (1966)
LEX BARKER (1949)	**RON ELY** (1970)
TOTO (1950)	**KARL BLOMER** (1978)
GORDON SCOTT (1955)	**ANDY LUOTTO** (1980)
MANCHAR (1959)	**MILES O'KEEFE** (1981)
DENNY MILLER (1959)	

THE PHANTOMS OF THE OPERA

LON CHANEY (in the 1925 silent version; director Rupert Julian)
CLAUDE RAINS (in the 1943 version; director Arthur Lubin)
HERBERT LOM (in the 1962 British version; director Terence Fisher)

'The Phantom of the Opera' is a classic horror/suspense plot, though surprisingly only filmed three times, as detailed above. The story tells of a potentially brilliant composer whose career is ruined and his face hideously scarred by acid. He vanishes to lead a twilight existence in the sewers below the Paris Opera House, from where he kidnaps a beautiful young singer as his vocal protégée, in a demented attempt to wreak his revenge upon the world with a musical triumph. The madman eventually sacrifices his own life to save the girl from death.

The lead character spends most of his acid-scarred period behind a mask, the removal of which provides the film's pivotal moment, as well as a test of the make-up man's skill. In this respect, the two remakes are little remembered next to the staggering impact of Lon Chaney's self-created make-up in the original production — a strong contribution to the legend which earned him the appellation of 'The Man With a Thousand Faces'.

The actresses portraying the kidnapped ripper-off of the mask in each of the three films were, respectively, Mary Philbin, Susanna Foster and Heather Sears.

Lon Chaney